To Live And Fight Another Day

By

Bracha Weisbarth

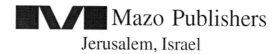 Mazo Publishers

Jerusalem, Israel

To Live And Fight Another Day

ISBN 978-965-7344-27-9

Published by:
■▮▰ **Mazo Publishers**
P.O. Box 36084
Jerusalem 91360 Israel

Website: www.mazopublishers.com
Email: info@mazopublishers.com

Design by:
𝔓**agemaster**

940.53
WEI

Partisan:

par'ti-zan, n. a member of a body of detached light troops making forays and harassing an enemy

About The Author

Bracha Weisbarth was born in the Ukraine in 1938. When she was three years old, the German Army entered and occupied the region where her family lived. To survive, her parents escaped to the forest with her, a sister, a brother, two uncles, an aunt, and a cousin, and then established a small partisan unit to fight the Nazi enemy.

After liberation, Bracha's family lived for three years in a Displaced Persons camp in Germany, before going to Israel in 1948, where she grew up. Bracha served in the Israeli Army and completed her education at the Hebrew University.

Bracha Weisbarth

The proud grandmother of five grandchildren, Bracha says, "My own children kept asking me how I survived the Holocaust – and I kept telling them little bits and pieces of what happened to our family during that terrible time. They were amazed to learn that there were Jewish partisans who fought against the Germans."

Bracha lives today with her husband in Morristown, New Jersey, where she works as the Director of Library Services at the Waldor Memorial Library. She is actively involved in the New Jersey Chapter of the Association of Jewish Libraries.

Dedication

This book is dedicated to my dear husband, children, grand-children, my brother Benjamin, and in loving memory of my parents.

This story has to be told. We must not forget the courage of the partisans. We have to keep their story alive so that everyone can learn about this aspect of Holocaust history.

My brother served as the model for Benny, the hero and narrator of this book, based on my family's survival. Benjamin was eleven years old when the Russian Army occupied the southwestern part of the Ukraine where we lived.

In 1941, two years after the Russian occupation, when the German Army occupied our *shtetl* (small village), all of the adult men were taken to labor camps. My brother became the man of the

Benjamin, the author's brother, riding his bicycle in their shtetl, before the war.

family. He foraged for food while we were in the ghetto. Benjamin saved our lives by forcing us to flee to the forest on the eve of the mass murder of the Jews in the ghetto.

BW

Table Of Contents

Prologue

I am sitting in the hot sun, looking out through the barbed wire of a British prison in Cyprus, thinking about the events that brought me here, more than one year after the war in Europe ended.

I am almost eighteen years old, an experienced fighter from my time with the partisans. When the war ended, I was determined to fight one more battle – for the Jewish homeland. I left my beloved parents and my little sister, also behind barbed wire, in a Displaced Persons camp in vanquished Germany. I set out for the Land of Israel to join the struggle to establish the Jewish State.

My plans came to an abrupt end along the coast of Israel, as British soldiers boarded the boat carrying me, my fellow survivors, and would-be fighters. We were captured and taken to this island prison.

Sitting here, my back to the dried-up fig tree, I remember the shtetl where I grew up. My beloved hometown became a place of degradation and fear during the war. I was made to feel like a stranger there.

I remember walking along the main street of Malinsk, trying to make myself invisible as I came face to face with three Nazi soldiers. One of them looked at the yellow star on my shirt. He pointed his gun at me, and shouted, "Stop, you dirty Jew, where are you going?" I stopped and tried to answer his question. My mouth opened, but no words came out. I pointed with my hand toward the train station, and a weak sound, a squeak, emerged from my constricted throat. The two other soldiers burst out laughing, as they, too, pointed their rifles at me and pretended to pull the trigger. "Run, you little swine," the first one shouted. I ran away as fast as I could, not knowing if they were playing a cruel joke on a Jewish boy, or if they really meant to shoot me. I waited for the shot to ring out. I felt helpless.

I remember so much more: the forest that offered shelter; the partisans fighting the Nazis; the friends and family I lost. I did my best to survive, to help my loved ones survive. I joined the fight against the Nazis. I did not feel helpless in the forest.

I remember...

1

War Comes To My Shtetl

On a bright June morning in 1941, the blue skies over my home, Malinsk, darkened. A black cloud descended into our lives. It was a cloud that seemed to last forever. The war came to our shtetl with the sound of roaring motorbikes, the stamping of boots, and the barking of orders. German soldiers, guns in hand, became the masters of our fate. I was thirteen at that time. Overnight, life as I knew it, changed forever.

Only a small number of Jewish families lived in our shtetl, located in the Southwest of the Ukraine in an area known as Volyn. The town's name was derived from *maliny,* the Ukrainian word for berries. Wild berries grew in profusion in the nearby forest. Malinsk was situated along a major and strategic railway that connected Rovno, the county seat, to Kiev, the capital of the Ukraine, some 390 kilometers away. The roads in this part of the Ukraine were unpaved dirt tracks, passable only during the summer and winter. In the spring and fall, they were thick with mud. The railway was the only means of transportation into the Russian interior. Trains carried men, cattle, merchandise, food, and gas. And during times of war, the train was the only means to deliver soldiers, weapons, and ammunition to the front. Keeping the trains running was of major importance in peace and wartime.

Next to the Malinsk railroad station were located the lumberyards, which were connected to the main railway by train tracks. The area's dense forests were a rich source of lumber. After the trees were felled, they were loaded on flatcars and sent to other locations. Many of the people living in Malinsk worked in the lumberyards or were involved in the lumber trade, my own family among them.

Isolated farms and small villages were located on the edge of the ancient dense and marshy forest, in this sparsely populated area of the Ukraine. Most of the inhabitants were of Ukrainian descent. They grew crops of potatoes, sugar beets and vegetables and raised livestock. A small number of Poles lived in the area, mostly in the larger villages. An even larger population of Jews lived there as well. They made their living as tradesmen, storekeepers, and merchants, trading in livestock and lumber. Malinsk was one of the larger villages in the area because it had a train station, and the weekly market was held in the village center.

My father, his father, and his grandfather were all born in this village. Our family, the Feins, owned a factory for spinning wool, a flour mill, a farm, and parcels of land in the forest.

We lived on a farm outside the village in two large houses. My grandparents, David and Reizl, my two unmarried uncles, Moshe and Shlomo, and my two young aunts, Feigale and Rivale, occupied one house. My parents, my two sisters and I lived in the other house.

Hershl, my father, was the oldest son. He was tall and strong, with a merry twinkle in his blue eyes. He used to come home from work at mealtime, give my mother a big hug and play for a while with us children. He would catch my two-year-old sister Sheindale and bounce her up and down in his arms until she squealed with laughter and her blond curls danced around her face. He would wrestle me down to the floor and tease me constantly, saying I would have to eat a lot more if I wanted to grow up to be as strong as he was. I was the only male grandchild in the family. Dina, my older sister, said I was a spoiled brat. During our play times, she would laugh with us, but wouldn't join the rough games. At seventeen, she considered herself a young lady and above such childishness.

My mother, Mania, had grown up in the city. She was well-educated, gentle, and refined. She hovered over us and watched our horseplay with a smile on her face. She greatly enjoyed the times when her whole family was together, playing happily. These happy times would not last long; they were brought to an end by the war.

My father and his younger brothers grew up on the farm. They were tall men, strong and brave, who did not have the time to devote themselves to study, because they had to manage the family properties. Being in the lumber business, they went often into the forest. It was their job to select the right trees for harvesting. They knew every farmer in the villages surrounding the forest, and every trail and glade in the forest. As the oldest son of the wealthiest family in the village, my father became the unofficial leader of the small Jewish community in Malinsk, and supported many social activities with his donations. Mother was very involved with the welfare of the Jewish children, and visited the sick and elderly members of our community on a regular basis. We had many relatives in neighboring villages and in Rovno.

Now that his sons were grown-up and able to take over his work, Grandfather David was finally able to retire and take up the study of the Torah. The tutor that he hired to teach his grandchildren, studied with him in the mornings. He used to sit in the warm living room, stroking his white beard, absorbed in his studies.

Grandmother Reizl, plump and gentle, was busy running the large household for her unmarried children. My lovely aunts, Rivale and Feigale, helped her with the housework. She always prepared something sweet and tasty for us grandchildren to munch on. Dina, my sister, was a year younger than her aunt Feigale. They both attended the same high school and were considered the most beautiful girls in our shtetl, admired by local young men and visiting strangers.

After school I would sneak into grandmother's kitchen and taste the wonderful dishes that she cooked. I liked to taste her fruit jams and jellies, which seemed to capture the sweetness of summer in their glass jars. My favorite dish was *teigalach*, a pastry cooked in honey. Although I was always picky about my food, I had a great liking for all sweet delicacies.

Mother used to complain that I was too skinny. She would warn me that I would not grow taller because I did not eat enough. Little did she know that my grandmother's treats were to blame for my lack of appetite at mealtime. She was right as far as my growth was concerned. I was short for my age. I did not resemble my tall father or my strong uncles. Rather, I took after my delicate mother, which led to my getting away with many pranks. I had the reputation of being somewhat of a daredevil with an active imagination and I led my friends into many mischievous adventures.

Life on the farm was happy and free of worry. In the morning, I walked to school, where all the children of the village – Jews, Ukrainians, and Poles – studied together. Some Jewish families did not want to send their children to a secular public school, but attending school was the law of the land and everyone had to comply. At school, we studied the Polish language and history because our area of the Ukraine was ceded to Poland after the First World War. Later when the Russians took over, we studied the Russian language and history. I spoke Polish, Russian, and Ukrainian fluently.

At home, I spoke Yiddish. In the afternoons, the tutor came to our house to teach us Hebrew and Torah – the five books of Moses. I worked extra hard during the last year, before the German occupation, preparing for my Bar Mitzvah. After the lessons, I had my chores to perform.

I had many friends among my classmates. During spring and summer, it was difficult for me to stick to my studies, and I sometimes played hooky. I preferred to play in the forest or swim with my friends in the small lake nearby. In winter, I spent my free time sleigh riding, skating on the frozen lake, or trying to ski on my wooden, homemade skis.

The German soldiers who came to Malinsk that June were not the first to invade our peaceful village. After the First World War in 1918, Polish Border Patrol units arrived and established an army camp on the outskirts of the village, right next to our farm. My Uncle Moshe served as an officer in the Polish Army. Then in 1939, when I was eleven years old, the army of Communist Russia occupied the area, taking over the Polish Army camp. My friends and I loved to sneak up to the fence of the camp, hide in the tall grass and watch the soldiers. Our favorite game was playing soldiers, marching about with wooden guns, saluting smartly, and fighting important battles. It was great fun and I loved it.

When the Russian Communists took over, our well-to-do family was branded as *kulaks,* rich landowners who were perceived as enemies of the people. We were in great danger because many kulak families were summarily shot or sent into exile in Siberia. We were lucky. Although all our properties were confiscated and taken over by the Communist state, at least we were permitted to remain in our own house on the farm. Although my father was appointed manager of the factory and the flour mill, his personal freedom was severely curtailed, and every move he made was watched.

I had to grow up in a hurry and take over some of my father's duties in order to keep our family safe. At times I delivered messages to farmers, carried packages to their houses, or collected rent from tenants who lived in an apartment house that belonged to my grandfather. When I was told to do something, I did not ask for explanations. I did as I was told, and learned early enough to keep away from the watchful eyes of the Russian officials.

Still, despite the Russian occupation, life seemed to go on as usual. The Russian soldiers were friendly toward us. I did not notice the concern of my parents and my uncles. I paid little attention to the mysterious coming and going of the men of the family. I was not aware that cows disappeared from the barn, or of the hushed conversations among the adults.

I turned thirteen in the spring. As the first grandchild to celebrate a Bar Mitzvah, a great celebration was held in my honor. Family members from far and near came for the festivities. Aunts, uncles, and cousins filled our house. There were so many of them that some had to stay with Jewish neighbors in the village. The guest of honor was Uncle Boris, an engineer and loyal Communist, who lived in Russia. Despite the fact that it was a time of war, my mother prepared a wonderful feast with the help of Grandma Reizl, my aunts, and our cook. What joy to be together, to play with my cousins, to receive gifts from our guests. Little did we know that this would be our last joyous family gathering and that most of those who had come to celebrate would never see each other again.

War came to our region and then everything changed. The Germans invaded our district and the bad times were upon us. We had to obey the orders that were sent out from German headquarters. All the Jewish men were ordered to work for the Germans. They were ordered to come each morning to the train yard and forced to work long hours loading lumber onto the flatcars. In the evening, the men were allowed to go home.

The Germans took possession of our farm and a house in the middle of the shtetl that we owned. They confiscated all properties and goods that belonged to the Jews.

Our entire extended family now lived together in one house. Very little food was available for the local population and even less so for the Jews. It was up to the women to somehow obtain food for their children. Some food they got by bartering whatever they had, exchanging a tablecloth for a few potatoes, or a cooking pot for a handful of vegetables. Bread was rationed, and we were allowed to buy a small portion at the bakery each week. Jewish children were forbidden to attend the village school. My mother became our unofficial teacher, and my grandfather taught us Hebrew. Most of the time we were free to play in the backyards of our homes. Only a few German soldiers were stationed in the village, but the Ukrainian collaborators in German uniforms supervised the workmen and enforced the new German laws.

It was a hard time for my parents, but they hoped that the situation would eventually calm down and we would be able to go back to the life we led before. Mother said to us "The Germans are civilized people. When the fighting ends, they will leave us alone." Things went on in this manner for close to a year.

Then one day in July, 1942, new orders were posted telling us to gather in the market square at noon on the next day. On this beautiful summer day, all the Jewish families gathered in the market square, which was surrounded by armed German soldiers. They looked so menacing and cruel. They shouted and pushed us around. One young soldier kicked my grandfather, who was unable to walk fast enough. The women cried softly, their faces pale with their young children huddled against them. The men stood next to their families, as if to protect them from harm.

A German officer dressed in black stood up in his car. In a voice that was loud and harsh, he read long German sentences from a paper, which he held in his hands. The words made no sense to me, even though I understood some German. Then my mother translated his words to the people standing around us. All able-bodied Jewish men were to walk to a lumber camp in the forest, where they would work as lumberjacks and fell trees needed for the German war effort. As for the women, children, and old men, they were ordered to leave Malinsk, where they had lived all their lives. They were to walk to the nearby town of Berezne, some twelve kilometers away, where lodging would be provided for them in a place where all the Jews would live from now on. We were ordered to go immediately to our homes, pack up some clothes and some food, and to come back to the square in two hours.

Panic set in and the crying of the women grew louder – and so did the shouts of the German soldiers, who kept yelling *schnell, schnell* (fast, fast). In a state of shock, each family ran home to gather clothes and food for the journey. My mother, a frail and delicate woman, found the strength to go quickly through our closets and make bundles of clothes for each of us.

Then she wrapped bread in a clean cloth, gathered some potatoes and apples in a sack, and gave it to me to carry. I was to go with my mother and sisters. I, who celebrated my Bar Mitzvah just a few months ago, and recited the words "Today I am a man," did not accept this role willingly.

"Mother, I am not a small child anymore, I will go with father to the lumber camp. Give this sack to Dina. She can carry it."

My father, who was busy preparing his own bundle of clothes and food, talking to his parents and his sisters, trying to calm their fears, turned to me and said, "Yes Benny, you are not a child anymore. That is why you must go with your mother and sisters, with your grandparents and aunts. You are a strong young man; you must help them and do everything that you can to protect them. I am counting on you."

Carrying our bundles, we walked back to the market square. Mothers and children cried as they hugged their fathers and brothers, not knowing when they would meet again. All the while the Ukrainian villagers watched this scene, some with tears in their eyes, and others with smug smiles on their faces. Among them were some of my classmates, friends I had played with just a short while ago.

We started our sad march to Berezne, to our unknown fate, accompanied by the shouts of the German soldiers. I kept turning my head, looking at the group of men walking in the other direction, the German soldiers pointing their guns at them.

We walked for a long time in silence, broken by deep sighs, the quiet sobs of adults and the whimpering of the children. Everyone carried a bundle. Even my little sister, Sheindale, carried a small bundle of her own and her favorite doll. We walked and walked for endless hours. No one paid attention to the beautiful trees or the fresh smell of the flowers growing beside the road. From time to time the German soldiers would shout, "Halt!" We would sink down to the ground, catching a few moments of rest.

The German officer rode in his car, trailing our bedraggled group. He was smoking a cigarette, paying little attention to the hungry and exhausted Jews. One of the women, a mother who carried two of her six children in her arms, fell to her knees, unable to walk any farther.

My mother dropped her own bundle and walked over to the officer in the car and said in German, "Please, sir, please, help this poor woman. Allow her to ride in your car." He looked at her with contempt.

"If you wish to help her, take her children and carry them yourself. I will not contaminate my car with dirty Jews."

Quietly, my mother distributed her own bundles among us, picked up one of the children and carried him the rest of the way, while the woman carried her other child. Whenever someone in our group could walk no more, those among us with any remaining strength would help him. As the road seemed to stretch endlessly, more and more of the women and children could not keep up with the group and lagged behind.

At last, darkness fell, and we were ordered to move to the side of the road to camp there for the night. This was a new experience for me, my first time sleeping outside, under a canopy of stars. At first, I could not sleep. The rustle of small animals moving in the grass sounded very loud and frightening, and the soft cries of the exhausted women and children seemed to go on forever. Finally, I fell asleep.

At dawn, the shouts of the German soldiers awakened us and we resumed our march. After what seemed an eternity, tired and miserable, we reached Berezne. We were herded to one of the poorer sections of this small town, a small area enclosed by a wooden wall – the Berezne Ghetto. One gate in the wall through which people entered the ghetto led to the road to the center of Berezne.

As we walked into the ghetto, other Jews stood along the road, silently watching our group arrive. They had been herded into the ghetto from the neighboring villages many months before us.

In all, close to 3,000 Jewish men, women, and children lived in this small, overcrowded part of town. Those who had come earlier invited friends and relatives to share their cramped quarters. Those who had no relatives were assigned lodging by the Jewish authorities in vacant rooms in decrepit buildings, two and three families to a room.

Our family of eight, my mother, sisters, and I, my grandparents and aunts were given one room to ourselves in a crowded building. This room was to be our new home.

All newcomers were given identity and ration cards and informed of the rules that governed life in the ghetto.

During the day, Ukrainian guards made sure that no one left the ghetto without a written pass. If we did have permission to leave, we had to be back in the ghetto by sundown, before the gate was locked for the night. We were prisoners in a prison camp. We had to obey these rules or be punished for breaking them.

The adults in the ghetto realized how bad things were. Their fear and sorrow showed in their eyes. They were dejected, not knowing what to do.

But I was young. For me, it was an exciting time. In the ghetto I met a group of Jewish boys, some of whom I had known before. Others were new friends. There was no school to attend and nothing for us to do. We roamed the streets of the ghetto, trying our best to escape the crowded rooms and the worried faces of the adults.

In the beginning, we were just kids with no responsibilities, running free, managing to have fun amid the despair all around us. We formed a gang, and I became their unofficial leader. We played various games, just like the ones I used to play with my friends in the forest next to our farm. But in a few short weeks, the time for fun and games came to an end. I had to face my responsibilities.

Soon, food became very scarce in the ghetto. It then became the responsibility of the older children to provide for their families. It was time for me to keep the promise I made to my father and take care of my family.

I helped my aunts, carrying the pails of water from the communal water pump. I ran errands for my grandfather, and helped my mother. Above all, I took upon myself to provide food for all of us by going to the market and bartering some small family treasures for food.

Adults needed special passes to leave the ghetto, but the Ukrainian guards paid little attention to a rowdy group of children running freely through the gate. We were free to come and go – an important key to our survival. We were able to sneak out some goods and exchange them for much needed food. I learned to run out of the ghetto, hiding some item of clothing or a small ornament under my shirt. On the outside, I would try to exchange it for potatoes or corn at the market. I did not look Jewish. My sun-bleached blond hair and my blue eyes that I inherited from my father, made me look like a gentile farm boy. I spoke Ukrainian and Polish perfectly without an accent. The farmers in the market never suspected that I was Jewish. Because they believed I was Ukrainian, I had an easier time than some of my friends bartering with the farmers for food. I also found it easier to come up with a believable story when asked awkward questions about the goods I was selling. I was blessed with an active imagination, and managed to convince any interrogators that I was telling the truth.

We lived this way for a couple of months. Occasionally, word would reach us from father in the lumber camp. He said that he and all the others were well.

Back in Malinsk, a former employee of father's, of German descent, named Mr. Kurtz had been appointed by the Germans to manage our woolens factory. From time to time, he would visit the ghetto and bring some food for us and fresh milk for my little sister. Whenever my mother thanked him, he would say, "Pan Hershko was always good to me and to my family. This is the least I can do in return." Pan Hershko – Mr. Hershko – was the name by which the farmers in the area addressed my father.

One afternoon late in August, this Mr. Kurtz came to our room, took my mother aside, and whispered anxiously, "Panni Mania, take your family out of here this very evening. Something terrible is about to happen tomorrow. Go to the forest – hide!"

Mother stood looking at him, unable to decide what to do.

"Where can we go? We cannot leave all our relatives and run," she said tearfully. He shrugged, unable to help her and hurried away.

She called the family together and told them what Mr. Kurtz had said. My grandfather said, "Grandmother and I are too old to run and hide in the forest. You children must go without us. Don't worry, nothing will happen." But my aunts and my mother decided they could not leave their parents behind. Dina, my older sister, told my mother, "If you don't go, then I will stay with you."

I realized that the next step was up to me. I was the man of the family now. I had to make the decision. I had to protect my mother and sisters, just as father had told me. I had to act immediately!

Without saying a word, I took hold of little Sheindale's hand and started walking toward the gate.

"What are you doing? Where are you going?" my mother cried.

"I am taking Sheindale out of here. We will go to the neighboring village and hide with Fedor." He was a Ukrainian friend of the family, who knew us well. "If everything turns out well, we will come back tomorrow."

I kept on walking. Mother realized that she couldn't do anything to stop me. She grabbed a kerchief, tied it in the fashion of a Ukrainian *babushka*, and followed me. Dina ran after her. We walked out through the gate unchallenged and kept on walking along the road toward the village where our friend lived.

Once out of town, I saw German Army trucks loaded with soldiers heading toward Berezne. This was a disturbing sight. I walked faster and faster in the opposite direction. Why were all these trucks going toward Berezne? What was the "terrible thing" Mr. Kurtz had warned us about? These were the thoughts that kept running through my mind as we walked on in silence, trying not to draw attention to our little group, trying to look like a village family returning home from the market.

Finally at sundown, we reached our destination, Hotin, where Fedor lived, and knocked on the door of his house. Mother told him that we needed to stay with his family for one or two nights because we were on our way to visit our father in the lumber camp. He agreed and made us welcome, offering us something to eat. Then he led us to the barn and told us that we could sleep in the barn loft on the freshly cut hay.

When he left, mother pointed to one of the cows in the barn, "This is Bielka, the cow that used to belong to your grandmother," she said. "When the Russians came to Malinsk, we gave the cow to this man for safekeeping."

"So this is what happened to all the cows that belonged to us," Dina said quietly, as though finally finding the answer to a question that had long been bothering her.

My mother explained that under the Communists, anyone keeping more than one cow would be branded "enemy of the people."

"So we gave all our cows, but one, to our Ukrainian friends for safekeeping," she said. "A number of farmers have our cows, and they owe us some favors."

Now, I also understood what happened to our cows, and why Fedor so quickly had agreed to take us in.

Sleeping in the sweet-smelling hayloft was another new experience for me. I slept very well that night. In the morning the farmer, Fedor, came to the barn, a frightened look in his eyes. "Panni Mania, Panni Mania, a terrible thing has happened. Early in the morning, we heard many shots fired. My boy ran to find out what happened. All the Jews of the ghetto, all the men, women, and children have been killed. The German soldiers shot them in the old graveyard of Berezne. Not one of them survived."

2

Escape To The Forest

S tanding in the barn, listening to the words of Fedor, our
world, as we knew it, came to an end.

"Are you sure? They're all dead? Not one survived? How
can it be?" We were in complete shock, unable to comprehend,
unwilling to believe. Grandmother, Grandfather, Feigale and
Rivale, my beautiful, loving young aunts could not be dead. All
my relatives? All my friends? No. No. It could not be.

"Do you know what happened to the men in the lumber
camp?" mother asked in utter despair, tears streaming down
her cheeks.

"I do not know, I do not know," said Fedor. "But you must
hide. The German soldiers will be looking for Jews in all the
surrounding villages. It is not safe for you anywhere," Fedor
warned.

Mother tried to control herself. "We will hide today in your
hayloft. You must send your son to the lumber camp in the forest to find out what happened to the men. Then we will decide
what to do."

"It is not safe to travel now," said Fedor. "The Germans
are stopping everyone on the road, searching for escaped Jews.

My son will go to the camp when it is safe. I'll send him in a wagon as if to bring wood from the forest. But he can't go alone to the forest; usually at least two boys go for wood. Someone should go with him or it will look suspicious. Benny must go with him." We could not question Fedor's decision.

Unhappily, mother shook her head in agreement to this plan.

We burrowed deeper into the fresh hay, trying to hide from the danger, from the terrible news. Mother was crying softly, trying not to scare my little sister, who was singing a lullaby to her doll, the doll she never parted with, that she had carried with her on the long walk to the ghetto, holding on to it as we walked out of the ghetto. Dina wiped her tears and said quietly, "I am older than Benny, I will dress up as a boy and go with Fedor's son to the forest."

I would hear none of this. "You don't know how to handle horses, you'll stick out as a sore thumb, and endanger us all. I will go – there is no other way."

With agonizing slowness, that awful day and night passed, then two more days and finally Fedor believed it was safe enough to go. His son Ivan, who was two years older than I, hitched the horse to the wagon, placed two axes and a hunk of bread wrapped in a towel under the seat, and we were ready to go. Fedor wasn't completely satisfied with my appearance. "Benny, you look like a city boy." He gave me some peasant clothes. "Here, put on these clothes and take off your shoes. You must look like a real peasant or you will be caught by the Germans."

I realized that from now on I could no longer be Benny the Jewish boy. If I wanted to survive, I must look like a Ukrainian farm boy who dresses in old work clothes and wears no shoes in the summer. I took off my shoes, put on the shirt and pants given to me, and I was ready to go. Deep in my heart I knew that I must do my best to survive, not just for myself but also for the sake of my mother and sisters.

Mother hugged and kissed me and whispered softly, "May God watch over you. Take care of yourself and come back safely." Dina hugged me silently and Sheindale said "Benny, bring me some berries from the forest." I jumped onto the seat next to Ivan and we were about to leave. But Fedor stopped us. He had had second thoughts about our going to the forest. He realized that it was too dangerous for us to go all the way to the lumber camp. He decided to send us only as far as his cousin's house in the village closest to the lumber camp. He instructed us to go to his cousin Pyoter and to ask for him to help us find out what happened to the men at the camp.

Meanwhile, as my father later told me, word of the mass killing of the Jews in Berezne, had somehow reached the men in the lumber camp in Polliane. At first no one would believe the awful news. Some of the men decided to run to Berezne to find out what happened to their families. My father, who was in charge of a group of men that included his two brothers, agreed that they must find out the truth. He was unable to believe that the terrible news was true. Although concerned about the fate of his loved ones, he realized that rushing into Berezne was dangerous for any Jew. They must proceed with great caution. He offered to go and contact a reliable Ukrainian farmer, a friend of his named Pyoter, and ask him to go to Berezne to find out what happened.

"If the news of the murder of our families is true, every one of us is in great danger," he said to the others. "We must save ourselves for the sake of our families. We must escape from this camp, run deeper into the forest, and hide." He said that his brothers, Moshe and Shlomo, would lead them to a safe place, and he would meet them later with whatever news he could gather.

That night a few of the men, including my uncles, escaped from the lightly guarded camp. As agreed to beforehand, my uncles took these men to a secluded place deep in the forest, a spot they knew well, and waited for my father's return.

My father had gone in the opposite direction, away from the forest. In the dark he walked to Pyoter's house on the outskirts of the forest. He arrived there safely and learned from Pyoter the tragic truth – All the Jews in the ghetto had been killed and buried in a mass grave. At this point, the Nazis and their Ukrainian collaborators were hunting for any Jews who had survived the massacre. No Jew was safe.

Hearing the awful news was a terrible shock for my father. He assumed that we were among the dead. To ease his pain and his sorrow somewhat, he felt a great need to recite the *Kaddish*, the prayer for the dead. Kaddish is usually recited only in the presence of a *minyan* – ten Jewish men. My father was alone in the farmer's house, but the need was so overpowering, that he walked out into the orchard, stood among the trees, and talked to them. "I need nine more men for a minyan. If men can turn into cruel beasts, trees can turn into merciful men." He walked from tree to tree, touched each in turn and said, "I name thee Abraham. I name thee Yitzchak. I name thee Yaacov. I name thee Yoseph. I name thee Benyamin. I name thee Yehuda. I name thee Reuven. I name thee Levi. I name thee Asher." After he touched nine trees, and gave them Jewish names, he declared, "Now we have a minyan. Let us pray, *Yisgadal Ve'yiskadash Sh'mey Rabbo...*" He recited the Kaddish for us, his own family, and for all the Jews of the Berezne Ghetto. When he finished he went back to Pyoter's house, and sank to the floor in observance of *Shiva*, the seven days of mourning.

Ivan and I had not encountered any difficulties on our way to Pyoter's house. As we drove into the yard, Pyoter came out of the door eager to find out who was coming. Recognizing Ivan, he invited us in. I entered behind him, and there, standing half hidden behind the door, I saw my father! He hardly recognized me in my disguise, but I ran to him and hugged him as hard as I could, happy and relieved to see him. What amazement and joy we felt at this miracle of finding each other alive and well! My father believed that his entire family was dead. I believed that the Nazis killed him in the labor camp. My father's joy when he saw me and heard that my mother and sisters were safe in Fedor's house, could hardly be described.

Of course his happiness came to an abrupt end when I told him the rest of the terrible news. He could not accept that the rest of our family – his father, mother, and sisters – were among the murdered Jews of Berezne. He cried with bitter tears and mourned their terrible fate.

We talked for some time while Pyoter's wife, Katia, bustled around us, doing her best to comfort us, serving bowls of thick, warm soup. After awhile, we decided that my mother and sisters must leave Fedor's house. They would be safer hiding in the forest.

Ivan and I drove the wagon back to Fedor's house bearing the good news. My mother was overjoyed to hear that father was safe. We loaded the wagon with hay, hid my sisters and mother in the hay, and drove back to Pyoter's house where my father was waiting for us. The joy of the meeting was shadowed by sorrowful grieving for the dead. But we were together, our whole family. My parents resolved never to part again.

Pyoter told us that any Jew caught by the Germans or by collaborating Ukrainians was killed on the spot. Knowing we were in mortal danger, we had to act fast, to find safe haven for all of us. We had to decide what to do, where to hide. The decision was clear: only in the deep forest could we find shelter, food, and hope of survival.

Pyoter gathered as much food as he could spare, as well as extra clothes and a blanket. My father knew that he needed a few other things to survive. He "borrowed" a cooking pot, a saw, a small ax, a small spade and some rope. Next he rigged a piece of harness and a small wooden plank, fashioning a backpack so he could carry my little sister. For the next two years he carried my little sister on his back in this carrier. His foresight proved itself over and over again, and helped to save our lives, as well as the lives of others.

The items he took with him into the forest proved indispensable. In the months to come the cooking pot allowed us to cook good, warm soup, using greens growing in the forest. In the winter when all the streams were frozen, we melted snow and had warm water. Anything warm, even water, was a lifesaver during the cold of the winter.

With the saw and the ax, my father cleared the way in the dense shrubs and cut branches to build a shelter for us, a shelter that blended in with the forest trees and hid us from searching eyes. With the spade he dug out roots, made trenches and performed many other necessary tasks, needed for survival.

As darkness fell, we stole out quietly into the forest with our meager survival kit, putting a safe distance between the village and us. The forest was safer for us for many reasons. The German soldiers were afraid to go into the deep forest because it was uncharted with many deep bogs that could swallow a man. Most of the local villagers were superstitious and believed that evil spirits lived in the forest. They would only enter the edge of the forest to cut wood for the winter and gather mushrooms and berries. The deeper into the forest we went, the safer we were. It also meant that we were at a greater distance from friendly villagers and the ability to obtain much needed food and clothing. As a result of these opposing needs, our life in the forest took on a special pattern that required constant movement. We would come to the edge of the forest to look for food, then go back into the depths of the woods for safety, never staying in one place for more than a night, moving again and again to find safety, and repeating this pattern over and over.

I will always remember my first few days in the forest. It was the beginning of September. The woods were green and thick, although some of the leaves were already turning to gold. In the forest glades, white, red and blue flowers grew in great profusion, carpets of flowers. Berries were plentiful. Succulent mushrooms grew in dark wet places, covered by leaves. Birds sang and small animals went about their business securing food for the fast approaching winter. Gray wolves lived in these forests but they proved to be much less dangerous to us than our real enemies, the Nazis, who hunted us. The quiet beauty of our surroundings prevented me from realizing fully the danger and the desperate situation that we would soon have to face.

When we first entered into the forest it was scary and exciting. After a long, long walk, that was especially hard on my mother, our little family group finally came to the prearranged meeting place. The men from the lumber camp were anxiously waiting for us, and for news about their families.

They heard what happened, they knew that the terrible news

was true but were unable to believe it. Some wept, repeating again and again the names of their loved ones, praying for their own deaths. Others cried in anger, seeking the one thing that from now on would give a new meaning to their lives: revenge.

I lit a small fire using dry branches that did not generate much smoke and hung the pot over the flames. The men, who had escaped from the camp with only the clothes on their back and who had eaten only uncooked berries for the last few days, drank warm herb tea and ate potatoes baked in the embers. It was an unbelievable luxury. While my mother and sisters rested, the men talked, planning a way for us to survive. I sat with them, listened quietly, and hoped that I might contribute something to their plans.

On that first evening, we asked many questions concerning our immediate future. How long would we have to hide in the forest? We did not know. Were we the only survivors, or were there other groups in the forest? We did not know. Would the Germans come into the forest with the help of the local villagers to hunt us down? We did not know. All the answers were hidden by the horrible situation in which we found ourselves.

We had to face the new reality of our life in the forest. We had to find the means to survive. We needed shelter to hide from our enemies and from the cold. We needed food, fire, and clothes. Above all, we needed guns and ammunition for our own protection and to inflict punishment upon our enemies.

Slowly a plan was formulated: we must contact some of the villagers, who were friends of our family, who would, it was hoped, supply us with food, warm winter clothes, boots and information

"I can go to the village," I said. "I can pass as a Ukrainian farm boy. I did it when I went looking for you, father, and I can do it again. I can get us food as well as other things." I was sure that I could carry out any task that I would be given. My father objected, but I reminded him that this was not the first time I had passed as a Ukrainian and that I was capable of taking care of myself and was not in any danger. I knew I could do it, that I could help our whole group. As a matter of fact, our desperate situation seemed like one great, exciting adventure to me.

For the moment, no decision was made, but we were alive, safe, and my family was together once more. From now on, we would exist from day to day, facing dangers, difficulties and constant threats to our lives.

To live, to survive, was our first goal. The next was to take revenge on our enemies, to kill those who had murdered our families and wanted to kill us.

3

Cold, Hunger, And Fear

The first few weeks in the forest set the pattern for the next two years. We knew that the forest was our friend; man was our enemy. Looking back, it seems ironic that we did not fear the wolves, the biggest predator in the forest, but instead feared our fellow man who hunted us down without mercy.

We could trust no one until we had real proof that the person could be trusted. Even the trust given to a person had to be reexamined again and again. Times were hard and one never knew what price might sway a trusted man to betray us.

In the beginning, our small group numbered eleven people; our family of five, my two uncles, Moshe and Shlomo, and four men from our shtetl who escaped from the lumber camp with my uncles. Leibl, a strong man of average height, had worked in our factory. His wife and his only child were imprisoned in the ghetto and perished there. Yosl, who was a slim young man with bushy black hair and merry eyes, was a devoted Communist who was sent by the Russians from Berezne to Malinsk to work with the young people of our shtetl and to teach them about Communism. His parents and younger siblings lived and died in Berezne. Avreml, his forehead permanently wrinkled, used to work as a bookkeeper in the lumberyard. The hard labor of felling trees sapped all his strength. He also lost his whole family in the Berezne massacre. The fourth man, Fayvl, was the *Shochet* – the kosher butcher of Malinsk. He was a very religious man, thin and small in stature. He had eight children, the largest family in our shtetl. Two of his sons were my friends. His whole family perished in the Berezne massacre.

At first the adults tried somehow to get through the days in spite of their deep sorrow. The realization of the fate of their loved ones caused despair and deep depression.

Three-year-old Sheindale was probably the only happy person among us. She seemed to consider our life in the forest as an ongoing camping holiday. In our daily wanderings, my father carried her on his back in the backpack seat he had fashioned for her, but she liked to walk and whenever possible did so. Walking, she would stray off the path and pick flowers as a present for mother, later she learned to look for berries and mushrooms. She clapped her hands in joy when she spotted a small animal or a bird, and she kept singing softly to herself in her sweet voice.

At times, it seemed that the very sight of her brought some solace to the sad men in our group. This childish happiness would soon be gone, taken away by cold, hunger, and fear.

The need to survive and find food dictated the pattern of our daily movements in the forest. We were very much like migratory birds traveling from one place to another, in a never-ending cycle, walking to the edge of the forest to be closer to the villages and to the fields, the source of needed food, then going back into the deep forest to escape the danger of being spotted by our enemies. When the food ran out, we repeated the cycle. We could never stay more than one or two nights in the same spot for fear of being discovered by the Germans and their Ukrainian collaborators. Later on, as we started to commit acts of sabotage against the Germans, our situation became even more perilous. The more we acted, the more the Germans were determined to catch us and punish us for inflicting considerable damage to them.

In most cases, I went on my own on food-gathering raids that were all carried out at nightfall. I had very good night vision, and being fast and small, could reach my destination quickly, lessening the danger of being discovered. I would sneak into a field or a garden, crouch among the rows of vegetables and dig out potatoes or pick cabbages as fast as possible, stuffing them into my sack, and sneak out again, unseen. I knew that I contributed my share for our survival, just like a grown-up. It was a good feeling to know that I helped our group by bringing food, even if this meant having to steal it.

Whenever father or I had to leave the forest, my mother and little Sheindale would stay behind. Mother hated to be left behind, to be separated from us for any length of time. She wanted to go with us, to watch over us, as though in this way she could ensure our safety, but she realized that she had no choice. She had to stay behind, hiding in the forest. She realized that it was safer for my father to go unhampered by the weight of Sheindale on his back, enabling him to move faster. She anxiously awaited our return. After every foray, our reunion was celebrated with tears of relief, a prayer of thanks to God, and when we were successful in bringing some food, a warm meal.

As time passed, life in the forest became harder and harder. Survival by all possible means for the members of our small group of refugees became our main objective. We were never completely safe from our enemies. We were never warm enough in the winter or dry enough in the rainy season. We never had enough food.

We foraged for edibles in the forest and also obtained them from the villagers who lived close to the forest's edge. It did not matter whether they gave us food willingly or whether we had to get it by other means. Each foray into a village, to get food, put us in mortal danger. This is how we lived for the next year, until we were forced by the circumstances to flee.

Surviving in the forest was ruled by the changing of seasons, which presented us with specific challenges and rewards.

Fall and summer provided us with a steady supply of food, but exposed us to greater danger. During these seasons it was easier for our enemies to penetrate into the deep forest and seek us out.

Winter meant hunger, cold, and snow. We had to watch each step we made so as to not leave any footprints in the snow. At times, after we had carried out a successful action against them, the Germans would send spotter airplanes to fly above the forest and locate massed footprints in the snow. They would bomb those areas and shoot at anything that looked suspicious. But as long as they did not venture into the deep forest, we were relatively safe.

Spring surrounded us with beauty and renewed hope. The warming sun revived us after the long spell of the terrible cold. The melting snow in the streams swelled the marshes around us, making them impassable for the Germans, granting us a measure of safety.

My father's knowledge of the forest, and his foresight in bringing along the few tools proved to be the most important asset to our survival. The cooking pot, the ax, and the saw, were the instruments of life. In time, most of the men in our group learned from his example and equipped themselves with similar tools.

Learning how to survive in the forest was important to us all. The first thing we had to learn was the skill of moving quietly among the trees, leaving no traces of our passage. Any sudden noise might alarm the birds nesting in the trees, causing them to fly into the sky, alerting a watcher intent on hunting down Jews. We had to learn how to creep quietly behind a small animal and catch it for our next meal. The ability to throw a stone accurately and hit a hare, a squirrel, or a wild duck seemed to come easily to me. Hunting small game or birds for food, became one of my duties. It added meat to our meager supply of food.

Father shared his experience with us. "Always try to sleep in an evergreen pine forest," he said. "For some reason, it is healthier for humans, and it affords a better shelter in the fall when other trees shed their leaves." We took his advice.

Because we were rarely able to bathe and lacked some vital elements in our nutrition, we all broke out in boils. My father, who knew the medicinal properties of many plants and trees, knew what to do. He applied a budding leaf from a birch tree on a festering boil and it healed. To cure a fever, he prepared tea from spruce bark. He taught my mother these age-old natural remedies and she applied these medicines and her compassion as she tended the sick among us.

During the summer, my father would point out any edible berries or mushrooms, and he taught us how to recognize the poisonous ones. "Look under the pine trees, the brown pine mushrooms are good, very nourishing," he would say "and so are the meadow mushrooms, hiding under the wet grass."

When Sheindale, who loved color, would pick a beautiful red-capped mushroom and show it to him, he admonished her gently.

"This red mushroom is a toadstool. It is poisonous, and if you eat it, you will have a big tummy ache."

We were all obedient students and learned to collect the delicious bounty of the forest, which nourished our hungry bellies. Little Sheindale was very proud to gather the sweet edible berries and drop them into the small basket that Dina wove for her. She would never put a berry into her own hungry little mouth because she understood quite early on that everything collected was meant to be shared by the whole group. As time went by, she changed also. From the happy, laughing little girl that she was when we first entered the forest, she had turned into a silent and serious child. She instinctively understood that loud chatter, singing, or laughter might endanger us all. She never complained or cried.

I remember one time when I was able to bring a small loaf of bread from one of the villages that I visited. The bread was cut into thin slices and divided among the members of the group. Mother, who knew that the next day might not be so good to us, that food might not be available, took one slice of bread, wrapped it in her kerchief and said, "See Sheindale, I will keep this bread for you for tomorrow."

"Mommy," Sheindale piped up, "I am hungry now, let me have the bread now." Then like the little actress that she was, she repeated the expression that she often heard us saying, "Tomorrow will take care of itself, God willing."

Wiping the sudden tears that filled her eyes, my mother gave her the last slice of bread.

Yes, we lived from day to day because at times it seemed to me that there might not be a tomorrow. We had to enjoy what morsels of food we had today. Tomorrow would take care of itself.

Each day at dusk, one of the men would chop down some branches, and we would erect a small shelter. Dina and I would collect broken twigs to start a fire. We were able to warm ourselves and make soup from the wild plants we had gathered or the occasional meat that we had hunted.

I was very careful to choose only dry wood for the fire. Dry wood created very little smoke, which was practically undetectable. Wet wood created heavy black smoke, which could betray our hiding place. We never lit a fire after dark, because it could be seen from a long distance. No fire after dark was the most important law of survival.

The danger to our lives denied us even what little comfort a warm, bright fire could bring.

It was early September when we first entered the forest. The first few weeks were kind to us, and we managed as best we could to adjust to life in the forest under my father's and uncles' guidance. Knowing that winter was fast approaching, we needed additional things in order to survive: warm clothing, a steady supply of food, warm shelter, and above all, we needed guns. Once again, planning and foresight proved to be our salvation.

In 1939, the Russians occupied our region. When it became clear that the Communist government would confiscate most of the family's possessions, my father and uncles realized that they had to hide any valuables belonging to the family if they did not want to have them taken away. The best way to do so was to bury anything they wanted to hide in the ground on our farm. Among the hidden items were extra men's and women's clothes, blankets, and sheets. They also buried the silver Shabbat candlesticks that belonged to my grandmother and my mother as well as some pieces of jewelry and a small number of gold coins. The most important items that they buried were two rifles and bullets. They had bought the guns from a retreating Polish soldier.

Whatever household goods and clothes they could not bury, they distributed among friendly farmers. Some of these goods were given as presents and others were given to them for safekeeping. Livestock was distributed in a similar way, with the understanding that the farmers would keep some of the animals for themselves and return the others when the political situation changed. In this fashion, the brothers created good will toward our family among our Ukrainian neighbors. All the farmers promised to repay with kindness what was given to them.

Now the time had come to dig out some of the hidden valuables, as well as to cash in on the good will of the farmers who were given goods and livestock.

This was a dangerous mission, for two obvious reasons. Firstly, we had to go to our farm, which was now occupied by a German family, to dig out the goods. This posed a great danger to those who went there. The second reason was just as obvious. Asking favors from the Ukrainian farmers meant exposing a member of our family to the danger of being betrayed by some of those same farmers, who by now felt safe to do so. As it turned out, some of them proved to be true and loyal friends, who willingly gave us whatever food they could spare and returned some of the goods given to them for safekeeping. They were also willing to give us shelter when it was needed and to gather information about the Nazi and the Ukrainian police force and pass it on to us. Others fulfilled their obligations with very little grace and only after being threatened.

Though dangerous, we had no choice. We had to dig out the hidden goods before the earth froze. We needed the guns and we needed the goods to barter for other supplies. Our surviving the fast-approaching long, cold winter depended on this.

At the nightly discussion, my uncle Moshe said, "Hershl, Shlomo and I know where the goods are buried. We will go to the farm to dig them out." It was clear to everyone in the group that this was the only choice. Yosl objected. "I want to go and help. It is not a good idea to send all three of you on this danger-ous mission," he said. "You are the most experienced among us. We survived this long, thanks to you, so at least one of you must stay behind." The others agreed with him. It was then de-cided that my father, Shlomo and Yosl would go. A heated dis-cussion ensued among the members of our group. Special care had to be taken before going to the farm. We needed to get up-to-date information about what was going on at the farm and in our village before any action could be taken. Only on the basis of such information, would we be taking the next step.

It was my turn to speak up. "Father, let me go and find out what is happening," I said. "You can stay hidden and wait for me in the forest. If it is safe, we could go and do what is needed." Once again a debate ensued, with my mother being vehemently against my plan. Naturally, she was very worried about my safety. She raised very clear objections to the plan.

"Benny, everyone in our shtetl knows you," she said. "You will be recognized and turned over to the Germans."

I tried my best to calm her fears. "Don't worry mother, I'll be very careful. I'll keep to the side roads, close to the forest, and I'll stay away from any place where my friends might see me. I'll go to the farm in the early evening when everyone is eating supper. I promise that I will hide if I see anybody ap-proaching. Don't worry, I will be careful and quick."

I knew that scouting the farm had to be done, even if it meant putting myself in danger's way. I was determined to do whatever I could to protect my father and his party from being caught by German soldiers. In the end it was decided that I would go to the farm, disguised as a Ukrainian farm boy and check out the situation.

We had previous information that, even though only a few German soldiers were stationed permanently in Malinsk, they made frequent inspection visits to the lumberyards. It was best to plan a sortie to our farm at such a time when the Nazi soldiers went back to their lodgings. I had another reason for wanting to go to the farm. Deep in my heart I hoped to see once again my beloved dog, Rex. He was given to me on my tenth birthday. When I got him, he was the cutest puppy I ever saw, and I loved him as much as he loved me. I raised him and trained him myself. He was my constant companion and took part in all my games and adventures. When we were forced off our farm, I had to leave him behind. Parting with him was very painful.

The next day, father, Shlomo, Yosl and I walked the few kilometers to the edge of the forest to a point closest to our farm. As dusk approached, the men stayed behind while I proceeded to walk toward the farm. I had to make sure that no German soldiers were visiting the new owners of our farm on that evening, and that it would be safe for the men to proceed with their plan.

I knew this area very well and could practically move around with my eyes blindfolded. It was, after all, my home turf where I played so often with my friends. Being sure of this fact was very encouraging, and I felt no fear.

I glided silently among the heavily laden apple trees in the orchard, approaching our house as close as I could. The last few yards I crawled on my belly. I was quite sure that no one saw me. I was about to get up on my knees when all of a sudden a dark form jumped on my back. My heart stood still. I uttered a muffled cry, expecting to be pulled up by the rough hands of my attacker. Instead, a wet tongue started licking my face and whimpers of joy emanated from the throat of my beloved dog, Rex. What a relief and what joy. I was so lucky that the German family kept my Rex and did not replace him with another watchdog.

Eventually, after scratching him lovingly behind his ears and uttering many words of endearment, I managed to calm Rex down. Even though I wanted to keep on playing with him, I had an important mission to accomplish. The safety of the men depended on it. I raised myself to the windowsill and looked inside. The German family was eating supper, enjoying their warm meal after their day's work. They were alone. There were no German soldiers sitting at their table. I felt sure that the family would not leave the house that evening to go outside. It was safe for us to do what we came for. I crawled away from the window with Rex following me part of the way. Making him leave me and go back to the house was very hard, but finally I succeeded, and he walked away with his tail dragging on the ground. We were both unhappy, but more important matters were at stake. I ran to the edge of the forest where my father and uncles were waiting. On the way, I grabbed a spade that stood leaning against the barn. I apprised them of the situation, assured them that we were safe, and gave them the spade.

Very quietly, we proceeded to the spot where the guns and valuables were buried. The men took turns digging while I stood guard. Soon enough, the spade hit a plank. Underneath was the buried treasure. Very carefully, with a grunt of satisfaction, father pulled out the oilcloth-wrapped packages. The long package held the two rifles and the bullets. The other package held the clothes and valuables. As fast as we could, we filled in the hole and put some shrubs over the freshly dug earth in order to conceal any trace of our deed. No one saw us, no one challenged us, but the feeling of danger was with us the entire time. We knew full well that just one bark from a dog, just one pair of hostile eyes, could mean the end of our lives.

Laden with our precious bundles, we walked back into the forest. I could not leave without bringing a little present for my mother or my little sister. "Wait here," I said to my father. Before he could object, I ran to our orchard and picked some apples, of which Sheindale was so fond. Then, as we passed near the vegetable garden, I pulled out a few carrots, radishes and potatoes from the soil. This was a present for my mother. I thought about the fine soup my mother would cook for us with these vegetables. Actually I wanted to take some eggs from the chicken coop, or a maybe even a chicken, but I knew that entering the coop would create a lot of noise, alert the new owners of our farm and put us all in mortal danger. I gave up the idea.

We returned to the forest, to the appointed meeting spot. Mother, Dina, Sheindale, and the other men were there, waiting anxiously for our return. With great pride, I handed over the fruit and vegetables to my mother, and gave the reddest apple to Sheindale who proceeded to eat it with a sigh of happiness.

The bundles were opened, and we all marveled at the wonderful things that we had brought back with us. Each member of the group was able to get a warm item of clothing. Now we had additional blankets to keep us warm. Father was especially pleased at the sight of the white sheets that we brought, because it meant that we could wrap ourselves in a white camouflage and move more safely in the snow. The men rejoiced over the two rifles and bullets. Having rifles meant that we now had the power to protect ourselves, the power to "persuade" unwilling farmers to cooperate with us and supply us with food. Above all, it meant that we had the power to fight our hated enemies, the Germans, and inflict punishment on them.

4

Dealing With Friend And Foe

News reached us that the killing of Jews in other ghettos of Volyn continued. We learned that by chance or by pure luck, a small number of Jews managed to escape the massacres. Some hid in the homes of gentile friends, where they were kept in secret hiding places and survived, thanks to these fine people. Others had to leave these temporary shelters after a short while. Tragically, we heard that many of the survivors were eventually discovered by local villagers and handed over to the Germans for the promised reward of two kilos of sugar and a kilo of salt.

A few of the survivors fled to the forest and hid there. They were alone and desperate. Most of them had grown up in shtetls surrounded by other Jews. They spoke Ukrainian with a Yiddish accent, which gave them away to the hostile inhabitants of the area. They were also unfamiliar with the forest and did not have the skills to survive there. Many perished that first winter for those reasons.

Some of them were lucky enough to stumble upon other survivors, form a group, and together do their best to survive under these terrible conditions. Survival was most important to those who still had the will to go on living, but in order to survive, they needed warm clothing, food, shelter, and above all, the companionship of other people. Loneliness and fear led to despair, and despair led to death.

Occasionally, we stumbled upon other Jewish groups wandering the forest, mostly men and young boys. Some had resourceful and determined natural leaders who led their groups into hiding in remote parts of the forest. These leaders infused the members of their group with hope and gave them a purpose for staying alive. When we met one of those fortunate groups, we exchanged information, food, and whatever else could be spared. The main topics of discussion were our chances of survival and the need to link up with the Russian partisan detachments, which in those early days were few and poorly organized. More than anything else, we swapped information about other survivors roaming the forest. It sometimes happened that a man heard that his brother, who had resided in another village and who was presumed dead, survived the killings, and was a member of another group of survivors hiding in the forest just a few kilometers away. Such news was received with great joy, while confirmation of the death of a man's family extinguished any secret hope that they might have survived.

Bands of Ukrainians roamed the forest as well. Some were Communists who escaped from the fate awaiting them in the hands of the Nazis. Others were bands of criminals – bandits who had to hide from the Germans for various reasons. They were united by their hatred of Jews, and killed Jewish survivors with impunity. We heard stories of such anti-Semitic bands that acted in this manner, showing no mercy for their fellow man. At times, they attacked even larger groups of survivors. They had the weapons to do so and wanted to kill as many Jews as possible. We did our best to keep out of their way.

During our wandering in the forest, right after the escape from the lumber camp, we would occasionally stumble upon a few of those miserable Jewish refugees who hid in the forest, barely managing to keep alive. We listened to their stories, the miracle of their survival in the killing fields of their shtetls. We took them in, shared with them what little we had, and in time some of them became valuable members of our group.

Our small group was especially lucky from the start because we had among us men who knew how to survive in the forest. It was also our good fortune that from an early stage, we were able to get guns, warm clothes, and food. We shared all the food and clothing among us, as well as the hardships that were part of our new way of life. Each member of the group could count on the help and experience of the others.

As our group grew larger, providing for the basic necessities of more people became the main concern of my father and his brothers, the unofficial leaders of our group. Finding a safe shelter for a large number of people was difficult and moving as a unit was more dangerous. The traces of a large group could be more easily detected by our enemies and bring destruction upon us all. The time came when we had to separate into smaller units in order to survive.

We kept in touch and when a larger force was needed for a military action against the Nazis, we would regroup. I was called to be a runner to tell the other units of important meetings.

It was decided that we would attack the municipal office of Malinsk. While we wanted to spread fear of the partisans' power among the villagers and the German soldiers, our real goal in the operation was to seize the typewriter used by the village clerk. We knew that a typewritten letter or notice would look more official than a note written by hand and we hoped that it would also convey our strength and abilities.

Three small groups, ours among them, got together and carried out the raid on the municipal office. I took part in this raid. We did not engage the Germans in a fight and did not fire our rifles, but the very sight of a large group of armed partisans emerging from the forest scared the villagers and convinced the village clerk to give us the prized typewriter. Some of our arms were actually fakes – hand carved wooden rifles that, from a distance, looked like the real thing. Dina learned to use our "liberated" typewriter to create official-looking documents and leaflets. Many times thereafter, we were able to obtain extra provisions, thanks to our fake typed document, which instructed some farmer to hand over to the holder of the "official" paper, some otherwise unobtainable item.

The first survivors we came across in the forest were two young sisters, Bella and Rosa. We found them one day in the forest, nearly two months after the destruction of the Berezne Ghetto. As we passed by a mound of piled branches, the branches moved and we heard the muffled sound of crying. Moshe, who was in the lead that day, stopped, raised his hand as a sign for all to stop, and crouched behind the nearest tree. He looked at my father and in a questioning gesture, asked him what to do. Father indicated that we needed to find out what was going on.

As I walked directly behind Moshe, he indicated that I start digging in the pile of branches, all the time pointing the rifle at it. When I removed most of the branches, which were covering a shallow hole in the ground, we saw the young women. At first, the men spoke to the frightened women in Yiddish saying, *"Mir zennen Yidden* – We are Jews." But then, we recognized the two dirty skeletal figures as the daughters of one of the shtetl's shopkeepers. They looked awful. They were emaciated, dirty, covered with sores, their clothes in tatters.

The terrible physical condition of both Bella and Rosa touched our hearts. Moshe led them to our shelter where we did our best to help them as much as we could. First, they ate with great relish the cold cooked potatoes that we had with us. Then my mother took two blankets and made a small enclosed cover. Rosa and Bella stripped off their filthy, lice-infested, tattered clothes and washed in the warm water my mother prepared for them. Meanwhile, Dina took their clothes and washed them in a nearby stream. She hung them on the bushes to dry. All this time, the young women kept crying and thanking us for our kindness. Eventually, being a little cleaner, a little less hungry, and much less afraid, they felt safe for the first time in a long while, and were able to tell us the story of their survival.

Before the war, they were accomplished seamstresses and made their living by sewing. On the day before the mass killings, they left the Berezne Ghetto to stay a few days at the home of a gentile woman who lived nearby, who hired them to sew some dresses for her in exchange for food for their family. When the fate of the Jews in the ghetto became known, the gentile woman hid them in her house for a fortnight. Then she asked them to leave because she feared for the safety of her own family. In many cases, those kind gentiles who hid Jews in their homes paid for their act of kindness with their own lives. The Nazis were merciless. The woman suggested to the sisters that they hide in the forest. They did so, unwillingly, having no other choice. They were much too afraid to seek shelter far from the forest's edge, so they dug out this shallow hole and hid in it. Together, they would venture out at night to the nearby farms, searching for something to eat.

As time went by, they became weaker and weaker from lack of enough food, until finally they were unable to leave their hiding place. They were resigned to their fate and waited for death. Rosa, the younger sister, told us that when she realized we were digging through the branches, she felt sure that this was their end. She thought that a Ukrainian peasant had found their hiding place and that he would kill them right then and there. "I was quite relieved that the end had come," she said, "because I could not go on any longer. I wanted to die. But when I realized that you were Jewish survivors, too, I knew that at last our awful misery had come to an end."

At first they were weak, miserable, and depressed with tears of sorrow for their dead family running down their cheeks. But as time went by, being surrounded by other Jews, without the immediate fear of death, both regained their strength and became capable and useful members of our group. They helped mother prepare food. Using their sewing skills, they mended our torn clothing and made a warm coat for Sheindale from an old torn blanket. Much later, Bella, who learned to shoot firearms, became a member of a partisan combat unit. Rosa became a skilled nurse, caring for the sick and wounded.

In similar ways, additional survivors attached themselves to us during those first months. Our group grew to fourteen members, among them two gentile men, Tadeush, who was a

Pole, and Gavrilo, a Ukrainian. Both escaped from the Germans, who captured them and intended to send them to a mining camp in Germany.

Sheindale was the only child among us. We were the lucky ones. The five members of our immediate family were the only family unit that survived intact. All the others were on their own, having lost their whole families. From the time they joined us, they considered our group to be their only living family.

Time passed and the members gained strength and confidence and some of their despair was replaced by a deeper feeling. They stopped thinking of themselves as survivors whose sole aim was to stay alive. Now, they found a common goal. They wanted one thing above all – to fight the Nazi enemy, to avenge the death of their loved ones and to help other survivors. They saw themselves as Jewish fighters, avengers, and partisans. I became aware of this change in their attitude while listening to what they had to say at our nightly discussions.

At night, huddling together in the dark, talk turned to the one subject that now was uppermost in their minds. They demanded action. These talks turned into planning sessions: what to do, where to do it and how. They were determined to fight the German enemy even at the cost of their own lives. This determination gave them the inner strength to hold on, to continue, and not give in to despair.

Even though I was only fourteen years old, I was a full-fledged member of our group and I took part in those discussions, fully committed to do my very best to help carry out our plans of revenge. Though small in size, I could offer my own special expertise, the gathering of information. It was very important to have information about our enemies before any planned action or raid could be undertaken. I volunteered to gather such information.

As we had only two rifles and very few bullets, I did not learn to shoot until much later.

Meanwhile, winter was upon us. As the group grew, we needed additional supplies. Father discussed matters with his brothers, and they decided that the time had come to call in some of the debts owed to them. I could not let such an action pass me by.

"Father, take me along. Four men are better than three," I said. "You know that I am able to help you." For a change he did not object. Maybe because I managed to accomplish many food foraging sorties on my own, I finally convinced him that I was a competent partisan. My mother, who was listening to my perspective of the plan, knew that her protestations to keep me from going would not help, so she kept her peace.

Armed with our rifles, we went to Kuznivka, a village located near the forest, to pay a visit to one of the Ukrainian farmers, a friend of our family.

It was dark. Most of the villagers were inside their homes, the livestock in their barns. We were free to approach the farmer's house undisturbed. Father knocked on the door.

"Who's there?" a frightened voice asked.

"A friend!" father answered in Ukrainian. "Open the door!"

Slowly the door opened. The peasant, Matwei, looked fearfully at us, then recognized father and exclaimed, "Pan Hershko. Welcome. Welcome!" He moved aside and we filed into the house. "Thank God. You are alive! We heard that the Nazis murdered all the Jews, may God put a curse on their souls!"

Father explained our situation to him in a few short sentences. He asked Matwei to give him some flour, potatoes, salt, as well as two coats and a pair of boots that were left with him for safekeeping. He also asked for some discarded clothes of Matwei's son who was two years older than I.

Matwei looked at father, and at my two tall uncles who were armed with rifles. Without saying another word, he went about fulfilling father's request, while his wife watched us silently. Then she went to the pantry and brought out a flask of milk and handed it to me.

"Take this for your little sister, the poor little thing," she said. We thanked Matwei and were about to leave because it was too dangerous to linger at length in this specific village as it was close to a main road. German patrols made a habit of dropping in frequently for inspections of the villagers' homes in order to confiscate food for their own troops. The villagers had no choice but to give them whatever they demanded. As time went by, the villagers got smart and hid some of their produce in secret storage places.

"Pan Hershko, be careful. Some of my neighbors cooperate willingly with the accursed Germans," said Matwei. "I heard that in the next village one of the farmers found a starving Jew hiding in his barn and handed him over to the local police who shot him on the spot." Father asked for the name of this farmer, and then we left.

We returned safely to our hiding place in the forest and father reported to the rest of the members what Matwei told us. Everyone in the group was shocked and angry. "We must do something! We must teach the Ukrainian peasants that Jewish blood cannot be spilled without fear of reprisal," Leibl said. After a short discussion, we decided to pay a visit to that peasant and teach him this lesson.

Two nights later, a number of men walked to the village where the accused farmer lived. They knocked on his door, and when he opened it, they grabbed and gagged him, and marched him quickly back into the forest. In the safety of the forest, they interrogated him. Eventually, he admitted that he turned the Jewish man over to the police. Our men declared him guilty of the crime and sentenced him to death. The farmer was shot and a note was pinned to his clothes saying, "Death to the collaborator! Punishment was executed by the hand of *Jewish Avengers.*" Father did not allow me to go with them on this particular attack. Knowing what the outcome would be, he wanted to spare me the sight of an actual killing. He told me afterwards what happened.

This was the first time that members of our group killed another man, albeit one who was guilty of a crime against Jews. With mixed feelings, the men walked back to our temporary camp. Some felt joy at being able to avenge Jewish blood. Others felt sadness about having to kill, but all agreed that this deed was necessary to set an example for the other villagers and make them afraid of retribution from Jewish partisans.

The execution of the guilty farmer moved our group into a new phase. From that time onward, besides providing for our survival, direct actions would be taken against our enemies.

Now that I had the right winter clothes to pass as a Ukrainian peasant boy, it was time for me to go about the business of gathering information for our group. In short, it was time for me to become a spy. Dressed in a tattered coat, rough trousers, a peasant cap, and felt boots called *valenky,* I was ready to go.

Mother hugged and kissed me and murmured a short prayer for my safety as Dina and Sheindale watched. Father walked with me and gave me some last minute instructions. "We need to have as much information about the Germans as you can get. We need answers to such questions as, How many come to this village? Which route are they taking? What vehicles are they using? How heavily armed are they? How many local policemen are on duty in the police station during the day and at night, and what sort of arms do the policemen carry? We also need the names of known collaborators and the names of peasants who informed the Germans about hiding Jewish survivors. This is a lot of material that you are looking for. Do not try to get every question answered," he said. "Above all, Benny, you must try to draw as little attention to yourself as possible. Stay in the background, and if you feel any danger, run for safety. Remember, son, that we love you and we want you to return safely to us. I will wait here for your return." He hugged and kissed me and sent me on my way.

This was my first real spying mission. I was completely on my own, in the daytime, moving among the villagers. This was very different from sneaking at night to a field and stealing vegetables. I promised myself that I would do my best, gather as much information as I could, and get back safely to my anxious family.

I walked openly on the road leading to the village, brandishing a thick wooden branch like a sword. I hoped that I looked like a real Ukrainian peasant boy going to the village on an errand.

I was afraid, but my excitement overcame my fear. It was market day in the village. Many farmers from outlying farms came to sell produce or wood and to buy provisions for their families. I mingled among the crowd, one among many, and sauntered toward the center of the village to the market place where, in the past, most of the stores and stalls used to be owned by Jews. Now Polish and Ukrainian shopkeepers took the Jews' places and served their customers. As I walked from one group of farmers to another, I kept my ears open for any tidbit of information. Some peasants were complaining that they could not buy the provisions they needed. Others cursed the German soldiers under their breath for confiscating their produce. They were very careful of what they said, but did not pay attention to a young boy who hung around, kicking dirt with his worn boots.

At a nearby stall, which sold potato knishes, stood two policemen enjoying this warm, tasty pastry. They were talking to a group of peasants standing next to the stall. "You see, life is much better for us now that the *Zhidy* (Jews) and the Communists are gone. Now we own all the stores and the stalls in the market. Soon, with the help of our friends, the Germans, we will finally be the masters of our land."

Some of the men in the group nodded their heads in agreement. Others just stood there without making any comment.

"Next week, on market day, the Germans will come here, and they will hand out prizes of sugar and salt to anyone who informs them about Jews hiding in this vicinity. Keep your eyes open for the *Zhidy*," one of the policemen said as he wiped his mouth and walked away.

I could not move away from this stall. I was hungry and cold, and the taste of a hot knish would be like manna from heaven. But I did not have any money. In the past, a boy could earn a kopeck or two by helping some Jewish housewife carry her packages while she walked from stall to stall. Now, all the women in the market were sturdy peasants who did not need help and who probably did not have a kopeck to spare. I saw a peasant buy a knish and bite into it. Our eyes met, and without a word, he broke off half of the crusty pastry and gave it to me. I mumbled a word of thanks and stuffed it all in my mouth.

Hastily, I followed the policemen back to their station. As

luck would have it, the chimney in the station did not work well and the policemen opened one of the windows to let out the smoke. I crouched underneath the window and listened to their conversation. Nobody seemed to notice me. Soon enough, I heard some very interesting news.

At that time, it was common practice for the German soldiers to raid any villages that did not deliver their quota of grain and produce. They would surround the village and conduct a house-to-house search. If they found any hidden food, they would take it, burn down that house, and send the owner to a labor camp.

The policemen told the villagers that next week the Germans would come to the village. They discussed the planned visit of the Germans. No surprise raid was expected here, because this village cooperated fully with the Germans. They mentioned that only a few soldiers would come from Kostopol, the nearby town. They would bring sugar and salt – rare commodities at wartime – as a special prize to reward informers and collaborators and to encourage others to do the same.

This was important information. I knew that the German soldiers would be traveling from their headquarters in Kostopol along the road closest to the forest. This was the only available way to this village. By now, I realized that I had achieved my purpose. I had important information to share. I had to get back to the forest and pass on this information to our group. We had to be ready for them.

I hung around the market for a little while longer. When some peasants started to leave, I walked behind them, seemingly one of their party. At a convenient moment, I walked to the edge of the forest as though answering the call of nature.

It is very easy to lose one's way in the forest, but father taught me an important lesson on how to find my way.

"Look at the trees, the tall straight birches and the evergreen pines. Do you notice something special?" he asked. I looked and looked and then I saw that all of the trees had moss growing along one side of their trunks. When I pointed this out to father, he was very pleased. "Yes, that's right. Moss always grows on the tree trunk on the side where sunshine does not reach it. This means that it is the North. By observing the trees, you can always find the North. Once you know your North, you can easily find your South, East and West. Knowing your direction in the forest will help you to find your way, and you will never get lost. Even in the dark, you can run your hand along the trunk and find the North." Following father's advice, I kept on walking for a time toward our designated meeting spot, deep in thought.

It's very strange, I reflected. Little Sheindale had an uncanny sense of direction. At a crossroad in the forest trails, she would point with her hand and say, "This is the right direction for us." She was always right.

Soon, I reached the spot where father was waiting for me. As we walked back to our shelter to meet the rest of our group, I told him what I had heard. Father praised me for the good job I had done. I could sense his relief and his pride in me.

That night, a long discussion ensued. We debated whether we were strong enough to attack the German soldiers. The pros and cons were examined. "If we succeeded in the attack, we would kill our enemy, take their weapons, ammunition and the valuable salt and sugar," someone said.

"What if we do not succeed? What will happen to the attacking party? We are taking a chance that we would most probably be killed," countered another.

It was a great temptation to act and a great danger as well. We had only two rifles. We were not strong enough for such an attack. After arguing for a long time, a plan was agreed upon. Next week, the attacking party would hide at the edge of the forest and wait for the German car. If conditions were favorable, they would attack. If the German unit consisted of a large number of soldiers, they would remain hidden and wait for another opportunity.

5

The First Winter In The Forest

It was late in a cold and wet October. The sky was gray. The golden leaves of the early fall dropped to the ground and formed a slippery carpet. So far it didn't snow, but the coming of snow was imminent. We continued our pattern of constant movement from one hiding place to another, not staying more than one night in the same place, careful to eliminate any traces of our being in a certain spot.

After my successful spying sortie at the village and the information I brought, the members of our group were very excited and determined. Here was a real and attainable chance to actually fight the Germans. We all started to prepare for action against the German soldiers on the road leading to the village I visited. We had to hurry with our preparations as we had only one week before the Germans were due. We had to make sure that we accomplished our goal successfully, without loss of life. Another reason for hurrying was the fact that an early snow might curtail our freedom of movement in the forest or cause the Germans to postpone their visit.

The next few days were dedicated to scouting out the area where the ambush would take place and picking the right spot for the ambush. The men made detailed plans of action to ensure its success and assigned each member to a specific place and duty. I was allowed to help my uncles clean our two rifles to make sure that they would function properly.

Mother, Dina, Sheindale, Bella, and Rosa stayed in a safe hiding place in the forest. Mother, once again, objected to my joining the fighting men, but my father explained that I was needed because I had a special task to perform. I was assigned to act as a lookout. I had to go up the road a ways, climb on a tree and alert the ambushing party about the approaching German soldiers. Father and I devised a few simple signals to convey information about the size of the German unit, how many rifles they carried, and how far away they were from the ambush. It was also my duty to warn the men if any other people were coming up the road. Based on signals, my father would decide whether to attack or stay hidden and let the German unit pass.

In the predawn hours we hiked to the designated ambush area. We did not know at what time the Germans would pass this place so it was better for us to be there ready to attack way ahead of them. Once we reached the designated place, the men hid beside the road, concealed by dense bushes that still retained many of their leaves. They stuck branches and grass in their woolen caps for extra camouflage and prepared for the long wait. Moshe and Shlomo, who carried our rifles, took their position at each side of the line, in front of the other men. Father was in the center of the group. I could see that all the men were anxious and tense. They tightly grasped their crude weapons, heavy wooden branches, which they had fashioned into sturdy clubs.

While searching for an appropriate place for the ambush, my father had located a tall pine tree positioned in a way that enabled me to see far up the road and still maintain eye contact with him. Once the men were in position, I walked to the tree, climbed up as far as I could, hid among the branches and prepared myself for a long, cold wait. Time passed, each minute dragging endlessly. As the sun rose higher into the sky, my tension grew. Suddenly, I saw a wagon hitched to a pair of oxen coming our way. I signaled my father that someone was approaching, but that this was not our intended target. The wagon was loaded with bundles of branches and cords of wood. It was just a peasant probably on his way to the market. Slowly, ever so slowly, the wagon passed our hidden group. Would the peasant notice something unusual? Would he discover us? The wagon kept on moving, but the peasant showed no interest in the bushes at the side of the road, and we all relaxed. In all likelihood, he intended to sell his wood before noon and then have enough time to return to his farm before dusk set in.

We had passed our first test, staying well hidden, unseen.

Later, I heard the unmistakable sound of motorbike engines. Evidently the diligent Germans did not waste time either. They meant to discharge their duties promptly. A moment or so later, I saw two motorbikes, with sidecars attached, coming our way. They were traveling side by side at a steady pace. The German soldier who drove it, hiding behind the windshield from the brisk, cold wind occupied the bike on the right. Another soldier sat in the sidecar. They were both muffled against the cold. A single soldier occupied the second motorbike, and his sidecar was laden with sacks.

In those early stages of the occupation, the German soldiers felt safe traveling unescorted, confident that no danger lurked beside the road. This confidence would change as more and more Germans were ambushed and killed on roads of the Ukraine.

I signaled father, indicating that two motorbikes holding three soldiers were coming. Father waved back acknowledging my signal and lowered his head. Shots rang out. Moshe and Shlomo fired their guns as soon as the motorbikes came to the spot opposite the ambush. This was the signal for the other men to rush out shouting and waving their clubs. The Germans were taken by surprise. The driver of the bike closest to our guns was hit, mortally wounded. The bike overturned on its side and the passenger in the sidecar was thrown out onto the road. He had no chance to draw his gun. He was stunned and apparently hurt by a bullet or the fall. The other driver seemed confused. He did not understand what was going on. He made a half-turn with his bike as though to investigate what had happened to his companions. His instinctive reaction cost him dearly. Another gunshot pierced the quiet of the morning and hit him directly in the face. He was dead before he hit the ground. The motorbike fell on top of him, wheels turning in the air. It was all over in a few seconds. From the treetop, I had a clear view of the ambush.

I climbed down hastily and ran toward the men. By the time I joined them, all three Nazi soldiers were dead. The men stood around the overturned bikes, cheering and slapping each other on the back. But there was little time. As previously planned, each man had a task to perform. While Moshe stood guard, one man took the guns from the dead Nazi soldiers and handed them to the other members of the party. Two men stripped the dead Nazis, and tied their clothes and boots into bundles. Other men unloaded the sidecar and distributed the sacks among the rest of the party. Father called me and instructed me to siphon out some gasoline and pour it over the bikes.

"But father," I objected, "these are good bikes. Let's take them with us."

"And what will we do with them in the forest, in the snow, without gasoline?" he asked me. He was right. We had no use for motorbikes in the forest. A burning pyre of German motorbikes, right in the middle of the road, would have a great impact on the Ukrainian farmers.

In short order, our party was ready to go. The men walked into the forest and disappeared from sight. Father gave me a match. I lit it and threw it on the gasoline-soaked bikes, which caught fire immediately. Then we, too, ran into the forest. The bodies of the naked German soldiers were left beside the road as a sign that German soldiers were no longer safe on the roads close to the forest's edge, where the partisans dwelt.

Laden with our booty, we walked at a fast pace deeper and deeper into the forest. We were elated by the success of our attack. We walked for a long time until we felt that enough distance separated us from the road and that we were relatively safe. It had been decided beforehand that we would not link up with the women for a day or two. This seemed a prudent thing to do in order to keep them safe. We had to be positively sure that we had left no traces that could lead our enemies to their hiding place and that we were not followed. At dusk, we stopped in a thicket among the trees and had a chance to examine our loot.

The German soldiers were armed with revolvers, two rifles, hand grenades, and ample ammunition. This was an unexpected bonus as it provided our group with much needed weaponry. I longed to be given a gun of my own, but I knew that the adult fighters needed them more than I did to use in future actions against the Nazi enemy. The six hand grenades that we now possessed were a welcome addition to our meager store of arms and proved to be a great asset to us. They would enable us to commit more attacks against our enemies. The sacks held sugar, salt, food, and two bottles of brandy. These provisions were worth their weight in gold because we could barter them for other goods that we needed. Another important item was a jerry can full of gasoline, even though it was very heavy to carry. Having gasoline meant having the means to start a fire quickly, even when no dry kindling was available. It was also a way to set fire to the homes and cars of our enemies. In time, we would learn to prepare firebombs by inserting a piece of rag into a bottle filled with gasoline, ignite it, and throw it at enemy targets. The Germans' boots, uniforms, and documents would serve our needs in the future.

We were tired, but elated. The men kept saying to each other, "We finally did it, at long last. We took a real step toward avenging the deaths of our families."

Now, after having passed this first test under fire, it would be easier for us to plan additional attacks. We spent two cold nights in the forest, afraid to light a fire, to draw attention to our temporary hiding place.

Two days later, we arrived at the place where the women were waiting for us. Once again the reunion was sweet, and the good news as well as the food was thankfully accepted. It was a good thing that we had food, because we had to lay low for a while. We were sure that the Germans would try to find and punish the people responsible for killing their soldiers. For the next few days, we walked deeper and deeper into the forest. We hid as far away as possible from the roads and villages.

As a matter of policy, the Nazis carried out all punishment of the so-called "criminals against the occupation" in public, to serve as a lesson and as a warning. Fear was a great deterrent for anyone planning actions against them. They always did their best to catch the guilty party and often punished innocent farmers when they could not find the real perpetrators of an attack.

Early in December the snows came. It was bitterly cold and snow kept piling up on the ground and on the trees. It was very beautiful, but very dangerous for us. We still kept moving from place to place, but now we had to be very careful not to leave any footprints in the snow. We walked in single file, and the last in the line dragged a pine branch behind him, erasing our footprints. One stormy night, we could walk no more. We were all hungry, tired and cold. The wind was howling like a wounded animal, and the snow kept falling as though someone was throwing it down on us with a big shovel. We tried to make ourselves as comfortable as we could under these conditions, but the snow-laden trees kept dumping additional snow on us as though they intended to bury us alive. Sheindale whimpered softly as she laid on the bare snow. Mother pulled out a blanket, unfolded it and tucked my little sister in it. Then, father unfolded a second blanket. He motioned my mother, Dina and me to take hold of one corner of the blanket and lift it above Sheindale, creating a temporary roof over her. As soon as the blanket grew heavy with snow, we shook it off, and kept holding the blanket above her, providing her with a shelter from the heavy snow. Finally the snowfall slackened, and we were able to huddle down beside her, cover ourselves with the blanket and try to restore some feeling into our frozen limbs. That was one of the worst nights in my memory.

It became evident that this would not do. We needed to find a secure place and dig in for the long winter ahead. After some scouting around, a suitable place that resembled a natural cave was found among the roots of a tree. We took turns digging deeper into the earth, and widening the cave. Then we cut down heavy branches from other trees at a distance from the location of our cave. These branches were placed tightly over the cave, and then we piled earth over the branches. On top of that, we piled snow and stuck branches in the snow to camouflage the whole structure. A small opening was left in the roof through which smoke from the fire could dissipate. A blanket tied with a rope to a frame of branches was affixed over the entrance and served as a makeshift door. It kept the wind and snow out of our cave, and did not let the light of our fire be seen from the outside. This structure, called *zemlanka,* Ukrainian for a house in the earth, was to be our home for the winter.

From the banks of a nearby frozen stream, we brought some fairly large flat stones, which served as a hearth for our fire. On this makeshift hearth, we cooked our meager meals and derived comfort from the warmth of the fire. Our underground home was very crowded, but surprisingly snug and warm.

The winter of 1942 was an especially bitter one, but this structure saved our lives. We were safe from intruders because the German soldiers did not dare go into the forest during the winter. Still, we had to be very careful because occasionally they sent airplanes to fly over the forest, trying to spot any signs of human habitation: clearings with footprints or trodden paths in the snow. Any suspicious spot was bombed and strafed with machine gun fire for good measure. We used extra care in keeping our dwelling from being discovered.

When one had to leave the zemlanka, one had to cover oneself with a white sheet, to blend in with the snow. One also had to drag a branch behind him to obliterate any footsteps. We could have a fire going, but we had to make sure that we used dry wood to eliminate thick smoke. Fire meant warmth and hot soup, but it also meant smoke stinging our eyes, which became red and irritated. Opening the door helped some, but then it got too cold inside.

From time to time, we had to sneak into nearby villages to

obtain food for the group. Two or three men would leave our hiding place at dusk, armed with guns, and walk in the dark toward a selected village. I took part in some of these raids. Once on the outskirts of the village, we would walk to a secluded house of a peasant and knock at his door. The startled peasant usually took his time before opening the door in the middle of the night, but he had no choice, knowing that if he did not open the door, his barn might be burned and his livestock taken. Once he opened the door, the men got inside. Food was a precious commodity at that time. It was well known that the peasants possessed hidden stores of food that they were willing to trade for needed goods. Our men offered to exchange sugar and salt for potatoes, cabbage, bread, and a piece of cured meat. In most cases this exchange was done peacefully, without trouble. Sometimes the peasant would add a small bottle of home-distilled vodka into the bargain as a sign of good will. As much as possible, we tried to deal with peasants who were known to be friendly.

Occasionally, we had to deal with someone who was known to be hostile to Jews, or a collaborator, or a policeman appointed to his post by the Germans. In such cases, the tactics were quite different. We would barge into the house and introduce ourselves as Jewish partisans fighting against the Germans. The man would be accused of being an enemy of his own people and of the Jews. We would tell him that this visit was an act of warning against future collaboration with the Nazi enemy. We would announce that we were confiscating some of his hidden food for the use of the freedom-fighting partisans.

Father took me along when he went to pay a visit to one of the peasants who owed him a favor. In most cases the peasants welcomed us, offering us something to eat right then and there, and gathered additional food for us to take into the forest.

One time we encountered a different attitude. We came to the house of a man who owed father a favor. Father and one of our men, Yacov, were armed with handguns, which were hidden under their coats. After knocking on the door, my father identified himself, and the door was opened.

The peasant stared at us with an unfriendly look in his eyes and barely greeted us. Father spoke politely. "How are you my friend? And how is your family?" he asked. He did not receive an answer. My father told the man what he needed, reminding him that he had been given a present of goods and a cow, but he only received a snarl in return. Then the peasant spoke up. "You damned Jews. You think that the whole world owes you something. Times have changed. If the Germans did not manage to kill you the first time around, they will soon catch you and kill you all. Get out of my house before I set my dogs upon you and call the policeman!"

Father's face turned red with anger. He reached under his coat and pulled out his gun, and Yacov did the same. Pointing his gun at the peasant, father said in an angry voice, "You stupid *muzhik* (a derogatory term for a farmer in Ukrainian.) You have an empty head and a short memory. You forget too quickly all the good deeds that my family and I did for you in the past. You forgot that when you needed medicine from the city, my wife got it for you. You also forgot all the things that we gave you, and that the cow in your barn belongs to us. No, the Germans did not kill us, and they will not kill us. We, the Jewish partisans, will avenge all the wrongs done to us. Now it is your turn to learn a lesson – one that you will not soon forget."

Father motioned Yacov to cover the peasant with his gun and then he ordered the farmer's wife and children to get up and get dressed. Meanwhile, we went into the larder and filled up the sacks that we carried with food. From the wardrobe, father picked out all the coats and suits that used to belong to us and tied them into a bundle. When we were ready, the whole family was told to come with us. We could not leave them behind for fear that they would alert the whole village to our presence.

"If you make any noise, I will shoot you," father said. We walked into the forest without being detected. After a distance of two or three kilometers, father stopped, "Take off your boots," he said to the peasant. "It is time for you to walk naked and barefoot in the snow, the way we Jews were forced to do by men like you. Remember, this time you are getting away with a warning because I take pity on your family. Next time we will not be this easy on you. We have guns, and we will be watching you. If, in the future you do anything to harm any Jew or partisan, you will be killed and your house will be burned. Now go back to your village, you ungrateful *muzhik.*" Trembling with fear and cold, the family turned and walked back along the trail we had left behind us.

"Let's hurry now," father told us.

"Benny, walk last in line and erase our footprints" were his instructions to me. I was so proud of my father who was just in dealing with the bad, but did not harm the innocent. I did as I was told, even though it was not easy to pull the branch behind me, laden as I was with a bundle of clothes.

Father is strong, I thought. Surely the lesson he taught the ungrateful peasant would not be forgotten. Word of what happened would spread, and it would deter other hostile peasants from harming Jewish survivors or antagonizing Jewish partisans.

6

Passover In The Forest

Our first winter in the forest was very hard, but we survived it, and now spring was here. Our zemlanka, the branch-covered underground bunker, had provided us with safety and warmth. Trading for food, or "liberating" it, kept the worst pangs of hunger away. Being part of a group provided us with friendship and support, a comfort for the wounded souls of our group. But the hardships of continued survival in the forest were immense and took their toll. Crowding in the tight space, our eyes constantly irritated by the smoke, the dirt, the lice which infested our hair and clothes – this was the price we had to pay for the comfort of our warm underground dwelling.

It was impossible to wash thoroughly either our bodies or our clothes during the winter months. As a result of the lice bites, we scratched ourselves constantly and some of the scratches became infected. The only way to cure such an infection was to boil a black ointment made of tree-bark and leaves and to apply it to the infected area. This ointment cured the infection, but turned our underwear into a black mess. Lacking any soap to wash our underwear, we had to turn to the only means that helped: boiling them in hot water and scrubbing them for a long time. This got rid of the black stains. My mother applied this black concoction to cure the infection afflicting our family and whenever possible, boiled and scrubbed our underwear while we sat wrapped in blankets waiting for it to be washed and dried. This was extremely hard work for my mother, especially under these harsh conditions. First a large pile of snow had to be melted into water in which to boil our underwear and shirts. Then they had to be scrubbed and scrubbed, until the skin of my mother's hands became raw. But she kept on doing this never-ending work, never complaining about this particular hardship. The rest of the group followed her example, using the healing ointment and boiling and scrubbing their underwear. She also did her best to keep our hair free of lice by rubbing gasoline into our scalps.

By now everyone in our group had some warm clothes, and wore boots made of felt, which kept our feet warm. But we were unable to obtain a pair of boots small enough for Sheindale. This was a real problem. Then, one member of our group, a cobbler by trade, offered mother a deal. He would fashion a pair of boots for my little sister from a worn-out pair of leather boots he owned. In exchange, my mother would clean and scrub his black, ointment-encrusted shirt for the rest of the long winter. Without hesitation, my mother agreed to the deal. She even sewed missing buttons to his shirt. In exchange, Sheindale got a pair of warm boots.

During the winter, we were unable to execute any additional attacks against the Nazis. Yet the resolve to fight them was never abandoned. Long discussions ensued in which different and imaginative plans were proposed.

By now we had a few things going for us. We had more guns and ammunition than when we started and we even had six hand grenades. We had gasoline to make firebombs, better known as "Molotov Grenades" or "Molotov Cocktails." Above all, we had more confidence in our ability to inflict harm upon the Germans, after our successful ambush. We were resolved to keep doing so, even at the cost of our own lives.

During this time, the war went on in the Ukraine, but at a slower pace because the harsh Russian winter hampered the German Army. Now that winter was coming to an end, one plan came to the forefront of all discussions and took precedence in our thoughts. We decided to derail a German freight train.

Because of the backwardness of the Ukraine and the harsh weather conditions, there were very few paved roads that could be traveled by cars. Trains delivered most of the soldiers as well as all the supplies needed by the German Army at the Russian front. Maintaining the rail system was of major strategic importance to the German Army, while disrupting the flow of men and materials to the front was a tactical necessity for the Russian side. It so happened that a strategically important railway line leading into Russia ran in the region where we were hiding. Our Ukrainian friends told us about the many heavily loaded trains traveling along those train tracks. With the coming of spring, the German war effort was renewed in full force, and they needed men and supplies. Their dependence on the rail system was complete. From our point of view, this dependence was the soft underbelly of the enemy. A great deal of damage could be inflicted on them with very little means and a lot of daring.

During one of our many discussions, Fayvl, who was the most religiously observant in our group, and did very little talking, said unexpectedly, "If I am right in my calculations, one week from today will be the eve of Passover, the night of the *Pesach Seder*." We were surprised by this announcement and saddened by it. Just a year ago, most of the men celebrated the Seder night together with their families, reading the Haggadah, eating the special Pesach meal, feeling the joy of the holiday which celebrated the Jewish redemption from slavery. And now...bereft, lonely, hungry, and in constant danger, how could we celebrate? A cloud of grief and gloom settled upon us.

Without thinking, I started singing the first of the four questions, "Ma Nishtana..." As I sang, Sheindale joined me in her clear and sweet voice singing the ancient melody, which she had not forgotten. Others joined us and soon we sang the four questions.

"We will have a Seder," my mother said. "It is not enough for us to survive death. Our survival, our life, must have meaning. We will celebrate Pesach as a sign of our eventual deliverance from our pain and suffering." Her words seemed to revive hope and determination in the hearts of the members of our group.

"Yes, yes, let's have a Seder," Uncle Moshe agreed.

"I can recite the Haggadah by heart," said my father.

"We need matzah for the Seder and wine and bitter herbs," added Bella.

"Bitter herbs?" asked Yacov. "Isn't our life bitter enough?"

The rest of the men ignored his comment and started to plan the Seder. A list of items needed for the Seder was drawn up, and the men set out to obtain as much as possible of what was needed. For the moment, the plan for the Seder took precedence over the plan for the train derailment.

It was decided that some men would go to a nearby Ukrainian village and obtain flour and food for the festive night. Dina pulled out a small silver pin that held her long braid in place and handed it over to my Uncle Moshe, who was among the men going to the village. "See if you can trade this in for some cherry wine," she said.

The men left. My mother, with the help of the two sisters, Bella and Rosa, set about to clean our zemlanka.

"This is as it should be. We always cleaned our homes for Pesach," Rosa said.

They ordered the men to wash themselves and to launder their shirts for the Seder night. When the men who had gone to the village returned bringing flour, wine, beets, and potatoes, the real work of preparation for the Seder began.

First, we had to bake matzah. A large stone was placed over the fire-bed, a fire was lit, and while the stone became hot, dough made of flour and water was prepared. With the help of a round piece of wood, Dina, Rosa, and Shlomo rolled the dough into round matzah. Sheindale was given a fork made out of a small bough and told to prick holes in the matzah. Mother placed the finished product on the hot stone, and after a short time, removed the baked matzah from this makeshift oven onto a clean sheet. I was kept busy with gathering more and more wood for the fire. Father and the other men erected a lean-to shelter made of branches next to the entrance to our dugout.

On the day of the Seder, my mother and the other women cooked the festive meal – hot beet-soup with some meat in it to add to its flavor, served with cooked potatoes. Somehow a few eggs were obtained and cooked for the feast, and a small bottle of cherry wine graced our makeshift Seder table, a white sheet spread on the ground. We did not have bitter herbs because as Yacov put it, "our life was bitter enough."

Sheindale managed to find a few early blooming spring flowers, to decorate the table for this festive occasion. We all sat around the white sheet, our Seder table, inside the lean-to, while my father recited the blessing over the wine, and we all took a sip from the small bottle. Our Seder was in full progress. We recited softly as much of the Haggadah as we remembered. Sheindale, the youngest, asked the Four Questions. We sang in muted voices the ancient traditional songs. We invited Elijah to come to our Seder and we ate all the special delicious foods with relish. Sheindale's eyes sparkled with joy while mother's eyes sparkled with unshed tears. For a moment, all our troubles seemed to have been lifted.

This Seder was a far cry from the grand Seders we used to celebrate in my grandfather's house as I remembered them. Each member of our group shared with us their memories of their wonderful Seders. But this special Seder had a deep meaning for all of us. After all, on this night we were free. We were together, and we upheld our traditional right to celebrate our holiday. Is this how our ancestors celebrated the Seder when they left Egypt? I wondered. Sitting on the ground, under a flimsy lean-to, eating unleavened bread, and thanking God for their deliverance?

The Seder was special and wonderful. It lifted our spirits and strengthened our resolve to execute our plan to derail a German supply train. As always, the first step was to obtain as much information as possible about our target, get a train schedule, scout

out the lay of the land and pick the best place for the derailment. We wanted to inflict a great deal of damage to our enemy, to disrupt the running of the trains for the longest time possible, and to try to achieve this objective without any loss of life to our group.

Once again, disguised as a Ukrainian farm boy, I was sent into Malinsk to the train station. I had to go in the daytime, when the station was open. On this mission, I was in greater danger than usual because one of our former neighbors or one of my schoolmates might recognize me. My father was aware of this danger and hesitated a long time before making the decision to send me into our shtetl.

"Look father," I said, "it has been almost a year since I was last in our shtetl. I have grown taller and thinner, my hair is longer, and I am really dirty. I am a Ukrainian peasant boy." Then another thought came to me. "No one knows that I am still alive. I am sure that no one will recognize me. Trust me, father, I will not be caught. I can run faster than all the adults in our shtetl, and I can beat up any kid who challenges me." This was a long speech. It seemed to have convinced father, or else he agreed because there was no one but me who had a chance to go and return alive.

My father made me promise one thing before going, which I did. "I promise not to go anywhere near our farm, and I will not try to find my dog Rex," I said. If anyone could recognize me, it would be Rex. We practically grew up together. He was my pet and playmate. I had taught Rex to perform a few tricks that he learned very quickly because he was a very intelligent dog. We were a great team. With my Rex around, I was not afraid of anyone. The bullies of our shtetl learned to give us a wide berth because Rex was ready to attack any bully who showed any signs of aggression toward me. What fine adventures the two of us had shared! Thinking of them made me smile. As much as I wished to have my old friend with me in the forest, as much as I wanted to see how he was doing, I knew that he might disclose my identity while showing his love for me, thus putting my life in danger.

Disguised and full of determination, I walked to the shtetl while my father stayed behind in the forest. Neither looking right nor left, I walked past the school that I had attended more than a year ago. Fortunately, school was in session and I did not meet any of my classmates.

I went to the train station, looking around me with great curiosity, as befitted a farm boy who is excited by the sight of an engine spewing smoke and steam and train carriages connected to each other like a long necklace of beads. I looked with admiring eyes at the assistant engineer, who perceived my admiration, and proudly showed me how he let the steam whistle blow by pulling on a certain switch in the engine.

"Oh, it must be wonderful to operate a train, to go to many distant places," I babbled. "How often do you go up and down this track?"

"Now that spring is here, we are very busy. We work around the clock. Every day five or six trains leave this station, and many more pass this way without stopping," he answered. "The damned Germans keep sending trains day and night, filled with arms and men. I think that soon the war will be over because they are so strong. They will win, and that will be the end for us all." His face clouded and resentment crept into his voice. "They are so sure of themselves that they do not even send out sentries to inspect the tracks."

I detected this hidden animosity and decided to take a chance. "What if the trains would stop going? Would the Germans still win the war?" I asked innocently.

He looked at me, winked and said, "If the trains stop, it would be very bad for them."

"If someone had information about train schedules, maybe something could be done," I said, knowing that by saying this I had put my life in his hands.

"The schedules for all the trains are kept in the top drawer of the stationmaster's desk, in his office," he said, turning his back to me and walking away. He knew well enough that giving such information to a stranger might be dangerous for him too, yet he had the courage to do it.

I decided that now, having obtained this important piece of information, I needed to get those train schedules.

I walked into the station and hung around the door leading to the stationmaster's office, hoping that I might have an opportunity to sneak in and steal those precious papers. I waited and waited, but the office was constantly occupied and I did not get a chance to go inside, much less get the papers. I was disappointed, but as the afternoon progressed, I knew that I could not hang around any longer. I had to leave. And so I walked out of the station and out of my shtetl, greatly disappointed.

When I got back to the forest, I apologized to my father about not being able to steal the train schedules. I felt like a failure. But when I informed him that German sentries did not check the tracks, he put his arm lovingly around my shoulder trying to console me.

"Don't worry," my father said. "You did well not to put yourself in danger. You need to understand that when important papers go missing, the enemy is alerted to danger and changes its tactics. We'll organize an around-the-clock watch right at the spot where we plan to derail the train. This way we will obtain the necessary information without alerting the Germans. At least, thanks to your report, we know that we can do all this without being disturbed by German sentries."

During that evening's planning discussion, it was decided that our next step was to locate a good spot for the derailment and post lookouts to determine the frequency of trains. We had to come up with a foolproof method for derailing the train successfully. After all, we did not have any experience in derailing trains.

The men got busy, walking stealthily along the tracks trying to locate the best place for the planned derailment, and learning the train schedules. Finally two things became clear to us. It would be best to derail a long freight train, and try to cause a great deal of damage to the train and to the tracks, making a quick repair of the damage impossible. At last, a suitable place was chosen. It was a bend in the otherwise straight stretch of track located on a high embankment. A clump of bushes grew right alongside this spot. This clump of bushes offered a good hiding place for our men, a place from which they could run for safety once the deed was done. It was decided that the best way to cause a derailment without using any explosives, was to dislodge a length of rail in such a way that, once the engine was traveling at a fast pace, and pulling a large number of cars, the supporting beams would be dislodged and the track would come apart. The first few cars would jump the track and fall down the embankment, pulling the rest of the long train with them.

We all agreed that this seemed to be a good plan, not too hard to carry out by a determined group of people. But I was a little disappointed. I kept hoping that we would put explosives under a bridge, blow it up, and then fire at the panic-stricken Nazi soldiers with our guns. This was just a dream of a boy who had a vivid imagination. The reality was that we did not have enough explosives to blow up a bridge, or enough men to ambush a train full of Nazi soldiers. Our method had to be different, less dramatic, but probably just as effective. We had to do the job quietly, decisively, and disappear afterward without leaving a trace.

I was very glad to be chosen to go with the party attempting the derailment. I was afraid that my father would leave me behind to guard the women. As before, my main duty was to serve as a lookout, to warn the men of any approaching danger.

A few days later, on a dark, moonless night, we walked the long distance along the forest trails until we reached a part of the forest closest to the spot we had chosen for the derailment. We were tired from the long journey. My father advised us to eat some food and to try to sleep.

"Tomorrow night we will have plenty of work to do. Try to rest now so that you will be at your best tomorrow," he said.

Despite our excitement, we took his advice. I was so tired that I fell asleep right away. We stayed hidden all that day until darkness fell. Then we walked quickly until we reached our target. My father told me to go farther up along the track and keep my eyes open for any sign of approaching soldiers. I was to give a loud whistle if I saw anyone coming.

It was a dark, still, night. I knew that I would not be able to see an approaching party until it was too late, but I could certainly hear one. The German soldiers felt so secure in their perceived strength that they did not bother to walk quietly. I knew that my services as a lookout were not needed. I decided that it would be best if I could help the men dismantle the rail.

Not wishing to disobey a direct order, I talked quietly with my father. "Father, listen, the German soldiers make so much noise that we will hear them from far away," I said. "Let me help with the digging. After all, another pair of hands will be more helpful than a sentry who is not needed. This way, we will finish our job much faster." I managed to convince him and he allowed me to stay and help the men.

On this night, as quiet as our party tried to be, we still made plenty of noise. Every sound carried a long distance. Anyone approaching could have heard the commotion we made, but it could not be helped. It was part of our dangerous mission.

From our previous observation, we knew that we had about three hours to complete our job before the next train was due. Some of the men, who carried crowbars they had "liberated" previously from a freight yard, started to unbolt the rail. After a lot of hard work, which took a good deal of time, they managed to lift a length of rail from the supporting beams. Then we dug under the beams until they were free, supported only in two spots, while the rest of the supporting gravel was removed. Next we put the rail back in place, and partially tightened the bolts.

At a glance, this part of the track looked just like the rest of the rail. We made sure that no telltale signs of our work would be visible and retreated into the nearby clump of bushes. We laid there, anxiously waiting for the train. Some time later we heard the clickety-clack of the approaching train. We tensed up. Would our plan work? Would the train derail?

The engine moved ahead, going full speed. One car, then the next and the third passed the loosened rail. Nothing happened. I was holding my breath, praying quietly "Let it happen, let it happen." Two more cars passed us. Nothing! Then slowly, like in a dream, the sixth car jumped the track, pulling the car behind it off the rails, then the others followed. We heard the sound of crunching metal. Heavily loaded cars tumbled off the high embankment, landing one on top of the other, making an awful sound. The scream of tearing metal sounded like the scream of a thousand dying animals. Then the engine, which till then was still moving slowly ahead on the track, started moving backward, ever so slowly, until it too rolled down the embankment. The shrill scream of escaping steam masked the screams of the injured Nazi soldiers. Suddenly, an explosion sent one of the carriages flying high into the air. This carriage must have been full of ammunition. Burning pieces of wood and metal fell all around, igniting some of the other carriages.

We had done it! We had derailed a German freight train! We were elated at our success.

It was time for us to leave, to disappear quickly. As previously arranged, we divided into smaller groups, and each group went in a different direction. We would meet later, in a safe place. Then we would celebrate our victory.

7

Escape Across The River

Elated with our success in derailing a German freight train, we were aware of the grave danger that this action put us in. To ensure our safety, we needed to erase all traces leading to our group and our underground hideout.

I was so proud of our achievement that I wanted to shout and tell the whole world about it! We, a group of hunted Jews, managed to derail the train using only our cunning and courage! I wanted to let our enemies know that we could inflict even more punishment on them in the future. Let them beware. Let fear enter their hearts. But this was just wishful thinking. Our strength depended on our ability to strike and disappear, leaving no witnesses.

It was decided beforehand that for the next few days, the combat group that took part in the derailment would seek temporary shelter deep in the forest. We would keep away from our hideout and not go in the direction of our safe haven, in order to confuse anyone searching for us. We would not lead our enemies to the place where my mother, sisters, and the other women were hiding. Only when it was deemed safe to return to our camp, would we go there.

The group divided into two-man and three-man units. Each unit was led by one of my uncles who knew the forest. Our unit consisted of Yacov, who used to live in Kostopol, my father and me. After saying a short goodbye to the others, the three of us beat a hasty retreat, running as fast as we could. We kept away from trodden paths, taking advantage of every thicket of bushes, traveling single file, trying to step from one stone to another whenever possible in order to eliminate our footsteps.

I knew that the next few days would be very hard. Our survival depended on our being fast and invisible. This meant that we had to travel light. We carried very little food. We did not carry any blankets or anything else that might have given us a measure of comfort, because it would slow us down. We all understood that if we had to suffer additional cold and hunger, it was worth it. I realized that this was my moment of passing muster – showing my father that I was a grown-up who could take these hardships without complaint.

It was early spring. The ground was wet and soggy, and the nights were so cold that the spring rains turned into freezing snow. We traveled at a fast pace during that day in order to put as large a distance as possible between the railway and us. At night, tired and hungry, we tried to find whatever shelter the forest offered to us in an effort to keep warm and dry. We did not dare light a fire. Yet, we were happy. We felt invincible. My father did his best to make the three of us a bit more comfortable. Whenever possible, he cut a few branches and erected a shelter where we huddled next to each other for warmth. He divided the food equally among the three of us, but somehow I always ended up with an extra piece of bread or an extra half of a potato. I knew where these extras came from – they were part of my father's own portion. This was his way of making my lot a bit easier. I was too hungry and too tired to object. But my heart was full of love, which seemed to give me extra power to endure.

While huddling in these temporary shelters, we kept talking again and again about the train derailment. Our success seemed to ease the discomfort of our miserable conditions. Yacov and I started making plans for future actions, each more daring and more dangerous. But father, ever cautious, tried to pull us back down to earth.

"The Germans will not take this derailment lightly," he said. "They will search for the perpetrators and do their best to catch them. Their punishment of the guilty will be public and very cruel. If no one is caught, they will not hesitate to punish the innocent. The Nazis have to set a terrible example to deter any future actions against them." He stopped talking, then after a few moments of thought he continued, "Right now we must be very careful. Our primary objective is not to be caught. Later on, when we regroup, we will consider the next step in our fight against the Germans."

Finally, after what seemed an eternity of misery, hunger, and cold, our small band started to walk toward our winter hide-out, taking as many precautions as possible, leaving no trace behind us, making sure we were not being followed.

As we approached the camp, we were eager to rush head-long and meet our loved ones, but once more my father was cautious.

"Benny," he said, "we need to know that we were not observed. We need to know that the camp is safe. You are our scout. Get as close to the camp as you can, climb up a tree and see what is happening there. Make sure to check all around to see if there are any suspicious traces around the camp. If all is safe, give us a sign by whistling twice. If something looks wrong or suspicious, you must come back here right away, without being seen. We will not make any move until we know for sure how to proceed."

I left them and started walking toward the camp, making as little noise as possible. My eyes scanned every bush, trying to see beyond it, trying to detect danger. I had to crawl on all fours in order to keep hidden. The smell of the awakening spring vegetation that I crushed pervaded my nostrils with the promise of an abundant crop of berries and mushrooms. As I neared the location of the camp, I kept looking for a suitable tree to climb to observe the camp.

Finally I found one and climbed up as fast as I could onto its lower branches. I kept as close to the tree-trunk as possible, trying not to shake the branches too much and making as little noise as possible. When I reached the highest point that I could reach, I looked in the direction of the camp. The campsite looked deserted. It was too quiet. There was no sign of life. My heart skipped a beat. What happened? Where was everyone? Did the Germans find our camp? Did the women have to run away? Were they safe?

Moments passed. The moments seemed like years. Panic gripped me. What should I do now? Then, a little figure came skipping into the clearing. It was Sheindale, cradling her doll. Right behind her walked my mother. They were safe!

I looked carefully around. No, nothing suspicious to be seen. I blew two loud, shrill whistles, and slithered down the tree trunk as fast as I could, almost falling and breaking my neck in my haste to reach the camp and hug my mother and sisters.

Soon enough, I was doing just that and being hugged in return. Father and Yacov came into the clearing. I knew in my heart that my mother must have said a prayer of thanks when she saw that we were back unharmed. She, too, must have spent anxious days worrying about us, not knowing what befell us, knowing that it would be a long time before we would return, a time that seemed longer because of the uncertainty.

It was best not to linger outside in the clearing, so we went into our zemlanka where we were served bowls of hot stew and cups of hot tea. I felt so relieved to be safe and warm, to have my whole family around me. I proceeded to tell the story of our heroic derailment of the train. The women listened attentively. I detected a look of envy on the face of my sister Dina as she listened to me. Then she whispered quietly, as though talking to herself, "Next time I will also go to fight against the Nazis."

During the next two days, the other men returned to our camp. We were greatly relieved that they, too, had made it back safely, but it was clearly understood that we were not yet out of danger. We knew that we could not stay in this relatively safe and comfortable camp, our winter home, for too long. We needed information that would indicate how things stood. We had to know how the Nazis reacted to the derailment and what their retaliation would be. We had to know what was happening in the villages adjacent to the railway. This was a job for me to find out.

By now, I hardly had to disguise myself. I looked very much like a Ukrainian peasant boy. Repeating our familiar drill, I walked to the edge of the forest, while my father stayed behind. We parted after agreeing on a safe meeting place. I walked in the direction of the nearest village, timing my arrival for the late afternoon when many villagers were returning home from their work in the outlying fields. This was a busy time of the day and no one paid any attention to a bedraggled boy who walked among the houses toward the center of the village.

The place was buzzing like a disturbed beehive. I walked slowly toward a group of men standing in the market square. They were talking about the one subject that was uppermost in their minds and which interested me most – the train derailment. All they wanted to know was who carried out this act of sabotage. Some of them gloated openly over the damage that the Nazis had sustained. Others were more guarded in their reaction.

"The partisans did it. They must have derailed the train," said one.

"They used fifty kilos of explosives," said another.

"Fifteen German soldiers were killed," said one.

"No. No. I heard from the policeman that ten soldiers were killed and fifteen were injured," said another.

"It will take awhile before the Germans clear and repair the train track," one of the men pointed out.

"What will the Nazis do to us?" someone asked in a worried voice.

"This is bad. Bad. We will all be punished," said another.

The men turned toward the door to a large house when it opened. An elderly man accompanied by a man dressed in a military-like uniform walked out the door and stood on the stoop.

"Let's hear what the village chief wants," someone said.

"Listen to me, my friends," he said. "We have received more orders from German headquarters." He took out a paper and read from it:

"The German military command declares that they will do everything in their power to catch the criminals who derailed the train. When caught, these criminals and their families will be punished by death. Anyone who has helped the perpetrators will be punished as well. Their farms will be confiscated and their houses burned. A prize of one kilo of salt and three kilos of sugar will be awarded to anyone who provides information about the criminals."

The village chief lowered the paper and continued speaking. "Now, we are commanded to provide a ten-man work detail to help with repairs of the track. Andrei, my deputy, will be in charge of this work detail. Anyone who volunteers for the work detail will be issued extra food rations."

The men listened to the chief. No one spoke, and no one volunteered. There were many reasons for their lack of interest in this offer. Some declined because, during springtime, there was a lot of work to be done on the farm. Some declined because they were afraid of retaliation from the partisans. Others did not volunteer because they did not want to help the Germans. The crowd, standing in the square, melted away as man after man sauntered away, seemingly set upon attending to more pressing business.

It would be left to the village chief to appease the Germans and to select ten men to fulfill their demand.

Under different circumstances, I would have whooped with joy at hearing this information. Two things were clear to me. One – even after more than a week since the derailment, the Germans did not have a clue as to who the perpetrators were. Two – the train track was still out of commission. The trains were not running. We really hit the Germans with a hard blow because they still could not transport supplies and men to the front. This was great news!

But right now I had to get away safely and warn my group

of the impending danger. This was not a time to linger around hoping to gather more information or trying to obtain some food. I walked away slowly from the square and made my way, as fast as I could, to the appointed meeting place in the forest. I told my father the good news about our success and about the determination of the Nazis to find the perpetrators and punish them. We walked quickly toward our hideout. It seemed to me as though I could smell the imminent danger in the air around us. We needed to get away as fast as possible from our hideout and find a more secure hiding place.

It was early the next morning when we finally reached the familiar clearing. The sentries who kept watch over the camp met us and assured us that everything was well. All of a sudden we heard the drone of an airplane engine. "Hide quickly!" some-one shouted. We took cover under the trees, hoping not to be seen from above, hoping that no one in the zemlanka would step out into the clearing. The plane flew overhead, made a wide circle and came back. Many questions raced through my mind. Had the pilot seen us? Had we been followed? Had we left too many traces of our existence in the hidden clearing? While these thoughts kept swirling in my mind, I prayed in my heart that the plane would fly away without detecting our presence.

As though in answer to my prayer, the plane made a wide circle and flew away. Behind the plane white sheets of paper floated in the sky like giant butterflies.

"Father, let me go and catch one of the leaflets," I said. My father nodded. I followed the floating leaflets with my eyes until I saw where some landed. Very carefully, I walked under the cover of the tree canopies toward one of the sheets of paper that had snagged on a nearby bush. I snatched it and went back in the direction of the camp. By then my father was entering the zemlanka. It was a lucky thing that no one had ventured outside the shelter at the critical moment when the plane was right over-head. I gave the leaflet to my father. It was written in the three languages commonly used in these parts: Ukrainian, Polish, and Russian. He gave the paper back to me and asked me to read it aloud to the rest of our group who gathered around us. This was his way of rewarding me for gathering the information in the village. This made me feel important.

The leaflet announced the very same message that the village chief had read to his men. This leaflet was further proof that the Nazis meant business. Our action really hurt them, and they wanted revenge. Additionally they had to punish the "Guilty Criminals" as they called the perpetrators of the derailment, in order to show the local population that they were in charge, and that they were strong and unforgiving. They would not and could not permit acts of sabotage in the future. Their punishment for such acts would be swift and cruel.

The search by an airplane made it very clear that we had to leave this safe place immediately. The Germans would never stop until they found us. They were as ruthless as bloodthirsty animals. We had to escape deeper into the forest. Once more, we would have to take up the life of nomad refugees. We knew that the warmth and comfort we found in our zemlanka would be a thing of the past. Fortunately, summer would soon be here, making life a bit easier for us.

My father drew a rough map of our immediate surroundings on the dirt floor of the zemlanka. He drew a squiggly line on the map, to the west of our present location.

"This is the River Sluszt," he said. "It is a fast-flowing river, especially now, when the melting snow is adding more water to it. We must reach the river without being detected and cross it despite the high and turbulent waters. The river is located some twenty-five kilometers west of this camp. I have heard that Russian partisans control the forest on the other side of the river. The Germans do not dare penetrate that area, but they bomb it frequently from the air.

"Right here," father said, pointing to a spot on his map, "there is a small dam that controls the flow of water in order to accommodate the needs of the flour mills below the dam. At certain times during the night, very little water is allowed to flow over the dam. This creates a shallow place of waist-high water. It is possible to cross the river on foot at that place." He looked around him at the somber faces of the group and continued trying to inject some measure of comfort into his words. "Remember, the dam is our target, but in order to reach it, we face a hard and dangerous trek. With God's help, we will make it, and we will cross the river to safety. Just as God split the Red Sea to save the Jews escaping from the Egyptian Army, so will He help us to cross the Sluszt and escape the Nazis."

I looked at the faces around me and I saw the deep worry and determination written on them. I asked myself, "Did any one of them regret derailing the train, which put us in this danger?" Their faces seemed to say that in spite of the danger, it was a worthwhile deed. There were no regrets, but the immediate need to find safety was the uppermost motivation to act swiftly. We collected what meager possessions we owned and started to select those most necessary for our future survival. Mother had tears in her eyes. This zemlanka had become home to her, a place where her family was warm and safe. Now it was time to leave it and head, once more, into danger and cold.

We had no time for sentiments or tears. My father assembled the carrier once more for Sheindale, while mother consulted with Dina as to what items to take, and what would be the easiest and most efficient way to pack and carry them. We could leave food, but not our arms, which would protect us if attacked by our enemies. All the guns and ammunition we had were distributed among us.

If and when we reached the river and crossed it safely, we would be on safer ground, under the control of the Russian partisans. Our arms would be our admission tickets into the partisan unit. Rumor had it that in most cases, anyone who wanted to join a partisan unit had to come equipped with a gun or a rifle, a token of personal bravery. Only then would he be considered for membership.

At sundown, loaded with our guns and bundles, we left our winter camp. Little Sheindale was perched on the carrier on my father's back.

Thus we began one of the hardest and most danger-fraught times of our existence in the forest since we first hid there. Before, we were shadowy beings who might or might not have been there. Now our enemies knew of our existence and would make the extra effort to find us.

As we walked westward for hours, daylight faded away and darkness descended upon the forest. Suddenly, we heard the drone of airplane engines. We scattered hastily and hid beneath the bushes, trying to find shelter. The planes seemed to be flying very low, almost right over our heads. I was very scared. All I could do was burrow deeper under the bushes, hoping to remain invisible.

Then, the darkness of the night turned into day, like a miracle from above, wrought by humans, not God. The Nazi pilots were tossing flares over the whole area. A white light, just like the light of a harsh sunny day, illuminated every tree in the forest. Such tactics indicated to us that our enemies must have received some information about a group of fugitives hiding in the forest, and they had come to flush them out. The bright light blinded me. I was very frightened. I was convinced that the Nazi pilot could see me clearly, despite the fact that I was hidden under a bush. Dina, who was next to me, was shivering so much that she made the whole bush shake. I was sure that this movement could be seen from above. We were in the bright light for what seemed an endless time, then one by one, the flares died, and the darkness of night was restored to us. A few moments later, flares illuminated another section of the forest, farther to the west. This time the Nazis must have seen something suspicious on the ground because I heard the deep boom-boom sound of detonating bombs.

As the sound of the airplane engines diminished, a strong sense of relief swept over me. Once again we were lucky. We had not been detected and had escaped the falling bombs. But fear did not leave us. We knew there would be other attempts to find and destroy us. There would be other dangerous "white nights," as well as dangerous days in which our very survival would be put to the test.

We kept on marching westward during the nights that followed, and slept during the day, hidden under thick bushes. The days grew warmer, but food grew scarcer. Our daily rations were cut in half because we did not know how long it would take us to reach the river.

One day as we laid hidden, resting after the long night trek, we heard the distant sound of dogs barking. To us this was an ominous sound. Once again, we felt like hunted animals, about to be located by bloodthirsty dogs, led by their evil masters. The men pulled out their guns and held them ready. If our enemies found us, they would pay a high price before taking our lives. We were all trained to shoot to kill our enemies, but we were also trained to keep the last bullet for ourselves. The Nazis would not take us alive.

Luck was with us once more. The barking of the dogs diminished in the distance, and we could breathe sighs of relief. The intensity of the search, as well as other signs indicated that we were getting closer to the river. We had to decide what to do next.

My Uncle Shlomo, who in the past used to deal with the owners of the flour mills in this area, volunteered to scout out the river and pinpoint the exact location of the dam. He would also check the times when the flow of the water was stopped. As a result of such updated information, we would approach the river close to the dam and cross it when the water level was at its lowest. It was a dangerous undertaking, but it made sense, and consequently, we all approved it. Without further delay, he started walking in the direction of the river, while we tried to conceal ourselves as best as we could, knowing that we would have to spend at least one or two days waiting for Shlomo's return.

The waiting period was long and tedious. Hunger gnawed at us, and we could not move for fear of being detected. Inactivity and boredom were hard for me, but more so for my little sister.

During those long and hungry days, when we did not dare move, we tried to amuse Sheindale by playing cat's cradle and other little games with her. My mother told her an endless number of stories and recited many poems, which she knew by heart. Soon enough, little Sheindale managed to memorize some of the poems and recited them back to us. It was very funny in a way to hear a four-year-old child reciting poems by Pushkin and Lermontov, the best-known Russian poets. She also had a very active imagination and played with her doll, which assumed different personalities at Sheindale's will. Actually she amused us and helped us pass the time.

At last, Shlomo returned. He had located the dam and told us to be ready to move toward the river when it would get dark. He said that at midnight the flow of water was very slow, and crossing the river would be possible. It was decided that some of the men would walk first, the women would follow them, and a group of men would guard our rear. Very carefully and quietly we proceeded in this formation. I was assigned a position at the front of the group, together with Shlomo who was to show us the way. My father walked next with Sheindale riding on his back, followed by my mother and Dina. The other members of the group followed them. A number of men were assigned as rear guard. As we came closer to the dam, we could hear the sound of the rushing water. This sound placed additional fear and doubt in my heart. Would we indeed be able to cross this swift river? Would we reach comparative safety on the other side?

We crouched under some bushes on the riverbank, waiting for the flow of water to stop. Clouds hid the moon in the overcast sky. We could see the dam, and we could see the maintenance building in which the switches, controlling the flow of water, were located. Shlomo told us that he knew that only one or two men were on duty during the night, watching the water flow switches. Knowing this made us feel safe and we did not expect any threat from them. As it turned out, the information, which was based on Shlomo's past knowledge, was incorrect. Because of the war and the strategic location of the dam, the Nazis installed a contingent of the Ukrainian militia in the building, unbeknownst to him. This unit had to guard the dam against acts of sabotage and to stop anyone crossing the river at this place in both directions. Mainly it was meant to be a deterrent against the Russian partisans who crossed the river from west to east and inflicted damage on the Germans. As it turned out, we paid dearly for not knowing this information.

After a short wait, the sound of the rushing water stopped. An unusual quiet descended on the river. This was our cue. It was time to move ahead and cross the river. We walked in a single file behind Shlomo. As we reached the shallow place, he motioned for the group to walk ahead while he stayed on the riverbank to bring up the rear. As soon as the first members of our group waded into the cold, shallow water, the clouds, covering the moon, moved away, and we were clearly illuminated against the dark water. Then all hell broke loose. A long volley of machine gun shots took us by surprise. The shots came from the vicinity of the maintenance building. The Ukrainian militia guards saw us trying to cross the river and opened up with concentrated volleys of gunfire. The people in the lead panicked, not knowing whether to keep going ahead or retreat. They were not able to draw their own guns and shoot back because the water reached to their waist and impeded their balance. For a moment, it looked as though this was the end for us.

I heard my father shouting, "Run! Run as fast as you can! Leave your bundles and save your lives! But then he said something, which I will never forget. "Whether I live or die, I can't drop the bundle on my back. I will not abandon my precious daughter. Everyone – hurry! Get across the river!"

The shots kept coming loud and fast. Someone screamed and then we saw a body fall with a splash into the water. Disoriented and confused, we did not know what to do. Then Shlomo's voice rang out. "Keep going. Cross the river! Rear guards, stay on the riverbank! Fire! Fire! Fire!"

That was the last time I heard his voice.

I kept running ahead, falling into the cold water and getting up again, praying for the shooting to stop, for the clouds to cover us in darkness. I hoped that the rest of my family was following me. I had no recollection of reaching the other side of the river. Suddenly I found myself on firm ground, running toward the bushes, breathless and afraid. When I gained the safety of the dense foliage, I stopped and looked back. I saw other figures running toward me. I saw streaks of bullets coming from the building, and other bullets coming from the bank on the other side. The loud noise of rushing water engulfed me. The water switches were thrown and a high wall of water came rushing down.

I could not tell if there were more people going across, whether they made it, or were swept away by the water. The shooting kept up for a while, and then it stopped.

Someone hugged me and I returned to the present. With great relief, I saw some members of our group crouching close to me under the bushes. Very softly, I started calling, "Mother. Father. Where are you? Answer me." To my great joy, I heard the voices of my parents and my sister answering me "We are right here. We are all right." Then my father said, "Right now, we must go deeper into the forest. Keep close to each other. Try not to get separated."

A short time later, we gathered at a distance from the riverbed. Quickly we counted our members. Most of the group made it across the river to safety, except for one woman and the three men who were the rear guard, my Uncle Shlomo among them. In my heart, I knew that we would never see these people again.

I knew that we made it to safety because, at the critical moment, Uncle Shlomo gave the order to shoot, and drew the enemy fire toward himself and his men. He gave his life to ensure our survival. He and his men died as heroes, putting the safety of the others before their own.

8

Linking Up With The Russian Partisans

Once across the River Sluszt, on the east side, we were now in a territory that was considered safer than our previous location. Here, as rumor had it, the Russian anti-Nazi fighters were in control. The Germans did not dare to venture into this part of the forest. The Russian partisans were well organized into a regular military unit and supplied with weapons by the Russian Army. This organization was in contrast with the bands of mostly Jewish fugitives who roamed the Irinovsky Forest on the west side of the Sluszt from which we fled. It was our goal to link up with this Russian partisan unit, to fight the Germans from within their ranks and gain a larger measure of safety, which was denied to us where we hid initially.

The loss of members of our group while crossing the river affected us all very deeply. This was the first time since we fled to the forest that we had to face the sad reality of losing friends and loved ones from amongst our own small group. We had been lucky so far. We realized that our luck could turn at any given moment, but did not experience it until then. Maybe we believed that having survived our first fall and winter in the forest, being able to live through the harshest conditions one could imagine, without any loss of life, and being able to inflict a blow against our enemies and avenge the killing of so many of our families, gave us a sense of false security. Now that we witnessed death amongst our own group, it was hard to accept.

We all grieved, but my father was heartbroken. He had lost his beloved younger brother, who gave his life to protect us. There was little hope that he might have survived.

The famous three Fein brothers, who were known as strong and honest men, had now lost one of their own. They were always close to each other during good times and bad. They were strong and brave, and could beat up any drunken peasant who dared to threaten them, or any of the Jews in our shtetl. Now Shlomo was gone. The chain was broken, but despite the loss, somehow the two remaining brothers had to go on.

Our situation had changed drastically. We were in a strange forest in unknown terrain. So, added to his deep pain, my father, being the leader of our much smaller group, was concerned about our survival, more than ever before. Here, on the east side of the River Sluszt, he was not as familiar with the surroundings as he was with the Irinovsky Forest, which bordered our shtetl.

In this forest, he did not know where the safe hiding places were located, a knowledge that had been key to our survival so far.

"We must try to locate the Russian partisans, and seek their help and protection," my father told us.

Sad and weary, our small group trudged slowly along a path that led away from the river and into the depths of the forest, alert to every unusual noise or movement. We were still hunted prey, and the vicious hunters would try their best to find and kill us. We kept on walking single file for many hours.

Father was still carrying Sheindale on his back. She clung quietly to his broad shoulders, never complaining, never asking for food, as though she, too, understood our grave situation.

I walked behind my sister, Dina. Despite my grief over the

death of my Uncle Shlomo, my active imagination did not rest. In my mind, I could picture our meeting with the Russian partisans, showing off the weapons we took from the enemy, and telling them about the derailment of the train. I was sure that now, being almost fifteen years old, I would be accepted as a full-fledged partisan. "Let it happen soon, let us find their camp soon," I prayed in my heart. I was sure that all the rest of our small group prayed for this as well.

I lost track of time. Suddenly, I bumped into Dina who had stopped walking. A figure carrying a gun stepped out from behind a bush and stood in front of my father pointing a gun at him and motioning him to stop. They stood looking at each other, each appraising the other. Not a word was spoken. It was a very tense situation. Finally the man spoke. "Who are you? Where are you going?" he asked in Ukrainian. He was dressed in a tattered winter coat, and wore boots made of felt just like the boots worn by Ukrainian farmers. A military cap was perched on his unkempt black hair.

Before father had a chance to answer, Dina stepped forward and exclaimed, "Yonah! You know me. I'm Dina. We were together in the Zionist youth camp." The man looked at her and recognized her. He lowered his gun and hugged her saying, "It is you! It is you! You are alive! I can't believe my eyes." Then he hugged my father and kissed my mother. He even tried to kiss me, but I would not let him do that. Obviously he was a very emotional man, but I felt that one has to draw a line on one's emotions. Kissing was for women. A second man holding a gun stepped out from behind a bush on the other side of the path.

How lucky for us that these men were on our side, that they were not members of some Ukrainian bandit gang. More importantly, that they asked questions before firing their weapons. In the forest, men had to be wary of one another.

For the sake of self-preservation, one had to be suspicious of other men. Hate and war turned men into enemies. For the sake of survival, one had to be very careful when encountering an armed stranger, not knowing what his intentions were, unable to give another human being the benefit of the doubt.

This encounter was yet another example of the dangers lurking behind the trees and bushes of the forest, an ever-present danger that dictated constant watchfulness and caution, required in order to survive.

"Let's not stand in the middle of the path," my father said. "Yonah, you must know your way around here. Take us to a safe place, and we will talk." Yonah conferred quietly with the other man, then he said, "Yes, I'll take you to the place where my family is hiding. It isn't too far. I'll have to leave you there and go back immediately. I am a soldier in the partisan brigade and I am on guard duty right now. I can leave my post for a short period, and my friend can do double duty until I return."

We collected our bundles and followed Yonah quickly. After awhile, we came into a small tree-shaded clearing. A hut made of timber nestled under the nearby tree. A tall woman stepped out of the doorway. She did not show any signs of alarm, probably because she recognized the man leading us. "Mother, it's all right. These are Jews I found in the forest. They need food and shelter," he called out. When he reached his mother, he hugged and kissed her. He certainly was a very emotional man!

More people came out of the hut and greeted us. It seemed unbelievable that this small hut could house so many inhabitants: an old man, three women and four boys of various ages, all younger than me.

Now it was my parents' turn to be amazed at seeing and recognizing one of the women. It was Rochel Mandel. She and her family were acquaintances of my parents. They lived in a neighboring shtetl not too far from us. After the German occupation, they were taken to the Rokitne Ghetto, but they were able to escape to the forest. Shortly after their escape, there was a mass murder of all the Jews in the Rokitne Ghetto.

As word about the mass killings spread among the survivors, they had no doubt about the fate of the Jewish population of all the other ghettos. Too few survived, so that any encounter with Jewish survivors was a joyous occasion. We marveled that at least another entire family had survived.

We were invited into their hut and put our bundles in a heap in the corner. Father took off the makeshift harness, and Sheindale got off his back. Very generously, Rochel and her family shared their meager food supplies with us. We were given hot tea, slices of stale bread, and some cold cooked potatoes. The warm hospitality of these wonderful people was the greatest welcome we could have received, after the ordeal we had just been through. This small and overcrowded hut offered us a taste of unbelievable comfort and security after days filled with danger, cold, and hunger.

Yonah took leave of his family and us to return to his post. After we settled down for the night, my mother and Rochel sat in a corner of the hut and told each other the story of their escape from the ghetto and their survival in the forest. Their stories were very similar in many respects. Rochel and my mother kept asking each other about the fate of mutual friends and acquaintances and wept with bitter tears over the brutal murder of so many friends.

My father had a different set of questions to ask. "How long have you been here? Are the Russian partisans helping Jewish survivors? How far is the camp of the Russian partisans? How much fighting is actually being carried out against the Nazis?"

Rochel's answers were like a ray of sunshine on a gray, stormy day. She told us that her family and other Jewish families, who lived in this small encampment, felt safe because this area was under the protection of the Russian partisans. On the whole, the commanders of the unit were reasonably helpful toward Jewish survivors and supplied them, occasionally, with food. Able-bodied men were welcome to join the partisan unit, especially if they had their own weapons. Women and children were not accepted into the unit, but were allowed to live nearby in what were known as family camps. There were several such camps in the vicinity of the main base. "Rest up a few days here with us, and then Yonah will come and take you to the base camp," she told my father.

In the Irinovsky Forest, on the west side of the river, small groups of survivors tended to put a distance between their hiding places. This was done as a precaution against being discovered by the Nazis or the Ukrainian collaborator bands. Any group of survivors that wandered into a territory occupied by another group was advised to leave the area and seek shelter some distance away. Often when a group grew too large it would split, one part of the group staying while the other part walked away to another location in the forest to find a safe place to hide. At times, such splits aroused feelings of betrayal and bitterness among the members of the group, but it was the most sensible road to follow in order to survive. However, here the situation was different. Being under the protection of the Russian partisans, many small camps existed safely in close proximity to the main camp.

Feeling safe and warm after our ordeal, we soon fell asleep in the crowded hut. We stayed with Rochel's family for a few days. Rochel was the undisputed leader of her group, which included four younger children, an old man and three women. During our stay, we were welcomed, in spite of the crowding and shortage of food. Sheindale found a friend in Dovidl, the youngest of the boys. They played together in a corner of the hut, giggling happily.

The old man looked very strange – his body, his face, and hair were covered with white dead-looking blotches. My mother, who was afraid that this might be some infectious skin disease, asked Rochel about it. Rochel told us that this man was taken with the rest of the Jews in the ghetto to the killing fields. "He stood at the edge of the mass grave and when the shooting started, he fell or jumped into the grave and was soon covered with the bodies of dead Jews. He was not hurt.

"During the night, after the killers left, this man managed to dig himself out of the grave and run naked into the forest. Other survivors who eventually found him wandering in the forest, helped him and brought him over to my hut.

"The blotches are not infectious," Rochel assured my mother. "They are the result of his terrible ordeal."

Finally Yonah came. He told us that he spoke about us with the Russian officers and, after some deliberation at brigade headquarters, he was instructed to bring us to the main camp.

As a rule, the commanders of the partisans were very suspicious of anyone showing up at their doorstep. They had to be very cautious. A Nazi undercover agent, posing as a fugitive, might endanger the whole camp by disclosing its exact location to the enemy, or by revealing plans for forthcoming operations against the Nazis. Therefore, any newcomers to the area had to pass the scrutiny of a trained intelligence officer. Any new recruits were regarded with a degree of suspicion until proven to be the real thing – loyal fighters against the Nazis. Often, they were not even allowed to join the main camp, but assigned to an outlying unit where their superiors observed them very closely. The proof that they were looking for was obvious. If the newcomers participated willingly in fighting against the enemy, showing courage and determination, they passed the test. Only then, after having proven themselves, were they fully accepted and trusted. Those who failed the test were killed.

Our group did not have to pass this type of scrutiny. We had two factors vouching for our true identity and loyalty. The first was that Yonah knew us personally and vouched for us. The second was that our group included women and children who were obviously Jewish survivors. So, as per instructions, we were brought to the main camp and presented to one of the officers. We formed a straight line hoping to present a military facade.

He looked at us, smiled at Sheindale, patted her curly head, and said, "This is a Russian partisan unit under the command of General Medvedev. I am Commander Kuzmitz. This is a military brigade, and if you become members, you will be considered soldiers of the Red Army. You will have to abide by all military laws. We heard about your courageous action in derailing the train and your other actions. Any member of your group with a weapon may join us. We won't accept women with children."

I was very happy to hear his words. After all, I had a gun

and I had taken part in actions against the enemy. Surely I would be able to join the unit and become a proper fighting soldier. Then another thought struck me. What about my mother and sisters? Where will they go? Who will protect them and provide for them?

Meanwhile, the officer walked along the line as though in a parade inspection. He stopped in front of each member of our group. He asked each one some penetrating questions about his immediate past and inspected his weapon. As he looked into the eyes of the person in front of him, his gaze seemed to penetrate into the very depth of the person's soul. Then, after a moment of reflection, he said, "Yes. You are all accepted. You may join us. You will be assigned to a platoon. The platoon leader will tell you what your duties are." Upon hearing these words, a bright smile spread on the faces of the men and women, who had passed this inspection, including my Uncle Moshe.

Finally Kuzmitz stood in front of our family and paused. First, he looked at my older sister and said, "So, you want to become a soldier? Do you know how to shoot a gun?" Dina looked into his eyes and answered, "Yes, Comrade Kuzmitz, I want to fight the enemy. I know how to shoot, and I am not afraid to use a gun." He smiled at her and shook his head in approval. Next he looked at me. "How old are you? Do you know how to shoot a gun?" My heart sank. I was aware that I looked smaller than my age. I was afraid that I might fail to be recruited, even though I felt like an adult and shouldered adult responsibilities when the need arose. "Comrade Kuzmitz," I answered boldly, "I am an experienced fighter. I can do many other things as well, and I am not afraid. I want to become a soldier." He seemed to like my spirited answer. "We shall see," he said. "We will have to find a special assignment for you. Meanwhile you are ordered to stay with your mother and little sister and guard them, until you are called to active duty." I felt let down, my hopes dashed. "But...but," I tried to speak forcefully, to make him change his mind, but he turned away from me and looked at my father.

"What about you, Gregory Davidovitch?" This was my

father's name in Russian. A look of deep concern crossed my father's face. "I want to become a fighting soldier, Comrade Kuzmitz," he said, "but I have my wife and children to consider. After the massacre at our ghetto where I lost my parents and sisters, I made a vow that only death would separate me from my family. I must stay close to them, to protect them. Please assign me to such duties that will keep me near to them. I want to become a soldier in your brigade and fight our enemies, but my first duty is to protect my family."

Kuzmitz seemed taken aback by this frank answer.

He scratched his head, thought for a few minutes and answered, "We need experienced and brave fighters. We do not abandon the families of our fighters. Your family will be assigned a place in a family camp. You will be able to see them as much as possible, but you must fulfill your duties as a soldier first and above all else. If this arrangement is acceptable to you, you are welcome to join our partisan brigade."

Under the circumstances, this was the best possible offer. My father could not refuse because refusal would have meant that our family would have to leave the protection of the partisan unit and fend for itself. He shook hands with the officer and I let out a happy cheer. Despite the fact that I was not really accepted as a recruit, I was confident that I would find a way to help and contribute to the fight against our common enemy.

We were given a few minutes to say goodbye and take leave of those members of our group who were accepted as members of the Russian partisans. From now on, they would live in the partisan camp. It was hard for me to part from them. We had gone through so much together. Would we see them again? It was even harder to take leave of Uncle Moshe. How could we part from him after losing Uncle Shlomo just a few days ago? We had no time to express all that we felt.

Then, the newly recruited partisans were asked to follow Comrade Kuzmitz. He instructed Yonah to lead my mother, my little sister, and me to the family camp, and introduce us to the camp leader.

My father saluted the officer and asked for permission from

him to be allowed to accompany us to the family camp, to see where it was located. Permission was granted, and Dina too, was permitted to go with us.

Once again, we picked up our small bundles containing all our worldly goods and followed Yonah to our next destination.

The family camp was located about a kilometer and a half away from the main camp. It contained about a dozen small huts, which were built under the protection of pine trees.

We walked over to the largest hut. An elderly man of medium build, wearing rough peasant clothes, came out of the hut. He looked at us with kind eyes and a smile spread on his white bearded face. He introduced himself in Yiddish. "My name is Rebb Yacov. I am in charge of this family camp. Welcome, welcome, it is good to see a nice family of Jews coming to join us. Who are you? Where are you from?" This time my mother spoke for us all. She gave him our names, told him in a few short sentences about us, and then she said, "Please find a place for us in this camp. We are in need of shelter, but we are able to work and contribute to the communal good of this camp." These were just the right words to say and they conveyed mother's deepest feelings. Rebb Yacov smiled, and invited us into his hut. "Rest awhile in here. I will locate a hut for you that is not too crowded, and you will be able to move into it. We need people willing to help in keeping this camp in good order. You will be assigned specific duties, once we know what you are able to do." He looked at my father and said, "Don't worry about your family. They will be as safe as any one of us. I promise you that we will share what we have with them. And you will be able to visit frequently."

Father and Dina, who were to go back with Yonah and leave us behind, hugged and kissed us. Once again, father told me to be the "man" of the family and to take care of my mother and younger sister. I nodded without saying a word. Mother, too, was very quiet. I think that she did not cry because she did not want to upset my father or any of us. She is strong, I thought. She will not upset or embarrass us in front of Yonah and Rebb

Yacov by crying.

Rebb Yacov was as good as his word. He checked some papers listing the occupancy in each hut and located one that was occupied only by three other people. "Yes, this hut is just right for you," he said. Then he gave mother some bread and raw potatoes from a storage shelf in his hut. "This food is your weekly ration. Divide it wisely because we do not have too much." Then he took us to our new home and introduced us to our new hut-mates. A new chapter in our life in the forest had begun.

9

Life In The Family Camp

It was accepted practice to disperse fighting units and family camps in close proximity to the main camp as a precaution against danger to the whole brigade. The Germans did not dare to penetrate the swampy forest, but they were able to bomb our camps from the air. The larger the concentration of people in one area, the greater the danger of being spotted from the reconnaissance airplanes that flew over the forest looking for the partisans. The danger was even greater during the long summer days when German soldiers were able to move with greater ease in the outskirts of the forest. During the summer, they mounted concentrated hunts for Jewish survivors and for partisans.

After each successful sortie against the enemy, we were in more danger than usual because the Germans were eager to catch and punish the partisans. Nazi airplanes buzzed the forest like angry mosquitoes and dropped bombs on any suspicious target. This danger dictated the daily life in the partisan camps. All members had to be very careful and keep hidden as a precaution against being discovered. Airplane spotters were posted on tall trees trying to spot planes coming our way even before their engine's drone could be heard. Very little movement was allowed in the camps during daytime hours. All the huts were built under the cover of tree canopies and were well camouflaged. No fire was allowed. Guards, from among the camp members, were posted all around the camps to make sure that no one could approach unnoticed.

Rebb Yacov ran our family camp strictly, but fairly. Our small camp was one among other family camps surrounding the main camp. Rebb Yacov, who was kind and easygoing, was very firm in enforcing the safety rules. He knew that our very lives depended on staying hidden from enemy eyes.

He also established rules of his own for all the camp members, based on his own experience. When walking from hut to hut, one must never go through the clearing. One must sneak among the trees, taking cover under their branches. Trampled-down paths were a sure giveaway to the existence of human beings in the forest. One must avoid walking along such paths at all costs.

All activities were to be carried out after sundown, including cooking and laundry. Wet laundry could not be hung out to dry in the open. It could only be hung on clotheslines inside the huts. Not only did that make our crowded huts seem even smaller, but the actual drying of the clothes took longer. Since most of us did not have a change of clothes, washing our clothes meant staying under a blanket until the clothes dried.

Another rule strictly enforced was that no dogs or other pets were allowed in the family camps. The main camp, he told us, had a large number of horses that were used by the partisans. But horses were not considered pets. They were the means of transportation from place to place.

Rebb Yacov explained all of the rules while we were walking to our new home. He made us promise that we would abide by them or face expulsion from his camp. We promised. He also told us that members of the family camp supported the war effort of the main partisan camp by performing various tasks as requested by the officers. When such a request came, we all had to do what was needed.

He introduced us to our three hut-mates: an old man, Baruch, and two women, Riva and her daughter Golda. Baruch wasn't related to them, but the war forged new ties among strangers, and for now, they lived in one hut. Rebb Yacov left us, after asking our new hut-mates to help us as much as possible.

The women, who were obviously glad to meet new people and have a new audience, told us right away the story of their survival. They kept talking and crying, talking and crying, as though by telling us what had happened to them, they would be able to cope with it.

Riva, a widow, had lived with her middle-aged, unmarried daughter, Golda, in Zirne, an isolated village. They were the only Jews living there. They owned a small grocery store. When the German soldiers came to Zirne, looking for Jews, the two women were too terrified to present themselves to the soldiers. They handed the keys to their store to a kind Ukrainian friend who hid them in his barn. They stayed in the barn throughout the winter. As time passed, it became too dangerous for their friend to continue hiding them. If he was caught hiding Jews, he and his family would be killed and his house would be burned. By the end of the winter, the farmer made contact with the Jewish partisans and arranged for the two women to join them. Riva and Golda were in no condition to be in a fighting unit so they were taken directly to Rebb Yacov's camp and have been there for more than six months now. They were both sickly and scared, but seemed to revive when meeting new people, and took comfort from those who were less afraid.

The old man sat on his bunk, barely acknowledging our presence. He did not talk at all, but when he saw Sheindale, he smiled at her. Later, we learned from Rebb Yacov that the old man, Baruch, was found by a detachment of partisans wandering in the forest, wounded and dazed. The medic in the main camp treated his wounds, and then he was sent over to Rebb Yacov's camp. The Nazis and their Ukrainian helpers murdered his whole family. He had somehow managed to escape from the killing fields. He seemed to live in a world of his own, hardly ever speaking.

I was quite unhappy being stuck in the family camp instead of being in the partisan camp with my father, my sister, and the rest of our group. Only one thing made the situation seem better. I was allowed to keep my handgun. Surely this was an indication that I was considered a fighting man.

Mother recognized my impatience as well as my obvious frustration and tried to help me to overcome it by pointing out the positive aspects of being in this camp.

"We will stay in this camp for a while. Thank God that we don't need to move each night to a different place. It will be interesting to meet new people, but don't be in too much of a hurry to go around to meet them," she said. "You will have enough time to do that later."

"Look at yourself," mother said. "You're dirty, and your clothes are dirty and so are Sheindale and I. First thing, as soon as it gets dark, I want you to heat some water for me. We will wash, and I'll launder our clothes. I want us to look our best when we meet our new neighbors."

At times, my mother still considered me her small boy who needed to be told to wash and look clean. This attitude irritated me. I was a grown-up man now, and I felt like a grown-up. After all, since the Germans invaded our shtetl and my father was taken away to the lumber camp, I acted as the man of the family.

Time after time, I had proven that I could take care of my mother and sisters, find food for them, and carry out many tasks as well as any adult. I was about to argue with mother, but then I saw the look on her face and kept quiet. I realized how terrible this new situation was for her. This was the first time, since we had escaped to the forest, that we were separated from each other.

Father and Dina were somewhere in the main camp, assigned to some unit, strangers she knew nothing about. She did not even know if the two of them were together, if they were safe, or when we would see them again. Now, she just had Sheindale and me with her. I knew that she was deeply worried, but she tried to hide it. She was also still grieving for my Uncle

Shlomo. He had survived the fate of the rest of our family and now found his death on the banks of the River Sluszt. He was the first casualty from among the original group of survivors. How many more might follow?

No, it would not be right to argue with my mother now and add to her worries. I shut my mouth and decided that I would get to know our neighbors later, even though I was very eager to become acquainted with them. I hoped I would find boys my own age, or someone I knew from the Zionist youth summer camps. I was eager to see new, friendly faces after living for more than a year with the same group of people. So I did as I was told. I resolved to help my mother as much as I could, but at the same time, try my best to get transferred from the family camp, and be accepted as a regular fighting partisan.

Our neighbors were eager to meet us, too, because any new arrival might bring some news from the world they once knew, news about the fate of their loved ones who had been left behind.

They came to our hut, introduced themselves, told us where they were from, and asked many questions about us. Where did we come from? How long were we in the forest? Did we ever meet so and so from such and such village? Did we hear about any survivors from such and such ghetto? Each question was asked in a trembling voice, as though afraid to hear confirmation of bad news, yet hoping to hear some good news. They told us their stories of how they survived, of the miracles that they experienced, of feeling guilty that the same miracle did not happen to their loved ones.

Many tears were shed at those first meetings. Since there were no other young children in this camp, the eyes of our neighbors followed Sheindale with longing, as though they were seeing their own beloved daughter, niece, or granddaughter. There were no boys my age in the camp, either.

In time, our new friends seemed to sense the inner strength in my mother's character, her sensitivity and goodness, and they drew as much comfort from her words as from watching Sheindale.

Rebb Yacov told us that the Russian Army plane, which

brought ammunition, medicine, and food to the Medvedev brigade, evacuated the wounded and mothers and young children to safety in unoccupied Russia.

"Mania, I will put your name on the waiting list so that you will be able to go to a safe place with Sheindale," he said.

"No, no." Mother objected. "We are going to stay right here, in this camp, as close as possible to my husband and children. We will not be separated. Whatever God has decreed to happen, we will go through it together. I feel safe enough right here in this camp. Now Rebb Yacov, tell me what I can do to help."

After some thought, Rebb Yacov suggested two tasks that my mother could do. Having learned that she was a pharmacist's daughter and had some medical training, she could be in charge of caring for the sick. The second task he suggested was to be in charge of baking bread for the camp.

He explained that this was not an easy job. He would supply the flour, yeast, and a large bowl for mixing. Her job would be to prepare the dough, and then take it to an abandoned Ukrainian village, some four kilometers away, where a working oven remained in one of the half-burned houses. Many abandoned villages were located in this area. She would have to bake the bread at night when no German planes were flying overhead. Then she would have to walk back four kilometers carrying the freshly baked loaves to our camp, to be distributed among the residents. This work had to be done once a week, and repeated week after week.

"It's a hard and dangerous job," he warned her, "but this bread is very important to us. The woman who performed this task previously is no longer able to walk the distance while carrying this heavy load. I will assign another woman to help you with the preparation of the dough. You will need some protection while walking to the village so I will arrange for Benny to be given a rifle. He will be your guard and go with you."

Mother agreed to perform both assignments on condition that Sheindale also be allowed to go with us to the abandoned village. Rebb Yacov accepted.

I was officially appointed her guard, but it was agreed that if I were assigned other duties, someone else would be given the rifle to guard the women going to the village.

From that time until we were liberated by the Russian Army, my mother, Sheindale, and Golda, who volunteered to help us, walked each week to the abandoned village to bake bread for everyone, and then walked back carrying the freshly baked loaves.

Let me tell you, there is nothing that compares to the smell of fresh bread, especially to a hungry boy. Sometimes I felt so hungry that I could have eaten all the loaves by myself.

Baking bread under those conditions was indeed a hard and a dangerous job. Walking on the open road leading to the abandoned village was especially dangerous. To avoid being spotted by an enemy plane or enemy scouts, we tried to negotiate these open stretches of the road as quickly as possible.

Even with my help, mother had to carry more than her share both ways because Golda was not strong enough to carry her full load. She also had to watch Sheindale at the same time, though she never complained. Even though I was the official guard and carried a rifle, I still carried as heavy a load as my mother and helped to keep Sheindale occupied during the long walk and the time it took to bake the bread.

Unlike my mother, I did complain. I wanted to be assigned to the main camp, to become a regular partisan. I wanted to fight, not stand guard over my mother while she was busy baking bread. I wanted very much the company of young people, not the women, children, and old men in Rebb Yacov's camp. In time, my wish came true.

When Rebb Yacov handed over the meager supply of medicine to my mother, our hut became the unofficial dispensary. Unfortunately there was not enough medicine to cure our ills. We were all undernourished. Our bodies were weakened by the harsh conditions of our life and we were unable to fight even minor health problems.

In addition to the usual colds which swept through our crowded huts, especially in the fall and winter, mother had to treat other medical problems, too. People suffered from skin rashes, infected mosquito bites, toothaches and headaches, to name a few of their ailments. The experience she gained while helping her father in his pharmacy was a big help for her as the unofficial nurse in our camp. For the severe cases, she was able to send the person to see the doctor in the main camp.

My mother reverted to using the medicinal herbs that grew in the forest and had been used by the Ukrainian villagers for generations. She brewed teas to treat stomach-illness, concocted ointments to treat skin rashes and bites, and used green leaves from trees to treat boils. She urged the people to wash their bodies and clothes as often as possible to prevent skin diseases.

Baruch proved himself an able and willing assistant. His help was most welcome, especially when she had to pull out someone's impacted tooth. He didn't talk much, but seemed more relaxed in the company of my mother and little sister.

We did not lack for company in our hut, especially after sundown, but I still felt quite lonely, yearning for the company of other boys. I also felt that I was not contributing enough to fight the enemy. How I longed to be with my father.

My sister and father came every so often to visit us. They were given permission to stay with us whenever there were no immediate planned military actions against the Nazis. On such occasions, it was great to be together again. Even Uncle Moshe, who was assigned to a small encampment farther away from the main camp, came to visit us occasionally.

As my father got to know our new location, he felt more at ease in this forest. He was appointed as the leader of a small scouting unit and sent on frequent missions. It was his unit's job to locate suitable places to lay mines, an ongoing effort to disrupt the enemy's mobility.

Fortunately, our life in the family camp fell into a routine, so my mother was able to think about something other than the enemy. She decided that it was time to teach Sheindale, who was now five years old, to read and write, but she had no books. She told me, "I heard that in Sosnove, the neighboring village, there is a teacher who runs the local school. I think that I will go there and try to obtain some teaching materials from her. I would also like to borrow a book for myself. I have not read a book since we were driven out of our home."

I started to protest. "Mama, this is a very dangerous idea. You could get caught and endanger all of us. Please don't go. It's not worth it."

But when mother made up her mind, nothing could make her change it.

"Don't worry, Benny, I will present myself as an educated Ukrainian from the city who is staying in Gorodisce, a neighboring small village, for the duration of the war," she said. "I will ask the teacher to lend me material to help me teach my daughter because there is no school to send her to in Gorodisce. No one will suspect anything."

Somehow, my determined mother found some clothes that enabled her to look more like the person she pretended to be. One day, dressed the part, she walked to Sosnove, instructing me to watch over my little sister while she was gone. She carried two loaves of bread wrapped in a piece of cloth and a basket of berries. I was terribly worried and waited anxiously for her return. The sun was about to set when I finally saw her coming toward me carrying a bag in her hand. I was very relieved to see her. At this moment, I understood how she must have felt every time one of us went away, and she was left behind waiting for our return. I kissed and hugged her, and Sheindale jumped into her arms.

"Tell me, tell me what happened," I asked excitedly.

Mother opened the bag. "Look at this, Benny. Mrs. Tchorny, the teacher, believed my story. She was very friendly. She gave me these books, Ukrainian primers, and some paper to teach Sheindale. She also let me borrow two of her books. I promised to return them to her in two weeks time, and then she said she would lend me more books. This is wonderful – to be able to read once again! Sheindale, darling, we will start your lessons tomorrow," she said with a smile.

Despite mother's obvious delight and trust in the teacher, I was not comfortable this arrangement. I was not sure that my mother's disguise was good enough and that her evaluation of this teacher was an accurate one. I resolved that next time I would go with her and judge the situation for myself. I was sure that my father would agree with me about this.

Meanwhile, mother started to teach Sheindale. My little sister was a bright child and seemed to absorb the lessons easily and quickly. My mother was happy with Sheindale's progress, and when my father came, Sheindale showed off her achievement as a student. He praised her for being a smart girl and learning to read. His praise made her very happy.

But he, too, was concerned about my mother's safety and tried to dissuade her from going back to the village. All his words were in vain as mother would not listen to him.

"Father, I have a plan," I said. "Next time I will go with mother. I will check out the place for any indication of danger. Only if I feel sure that this is not a trap, will mother go and meet this woman." Both my parents agreed that this was a good plan.

A few days before the two weeks were up, dressed once more as a peasant boy, carrying my gun hidden under my shirt, I walked with mother to the village while Riva and Golda watched Sheindale.

My mother stayed behind while I walked into the village. I looked around and tried to check out a few important signs that might indicate a hidden danger.

Are there any German soldiers in the village? Where is the policeman's house? Is he at home? Does the teacher's house seem suspiciously quiet? Where is the watchdog that usually guards the villagers' houses? I tried not to be too conspicuous while making these observations. As it was summer, the windows were open and I could look inside.

Everything seemed fine. I turned back toward the forest where my mother was waiting for me. She was carrying a small present for the teacher and the two books she borrowed. I told her that everything seemed all right. She walked toward the village. Now it was my turn to hide and wait for her return.

After what seemed a long time, I saw mother walking toward my hiding place. I called out softly and then joined her.

"I think that this will be the last time I'll come here," she said. "Mrs. Tchorny was very friendly again, but I could detect something in her eyes that I did not like. She kept asking me a lot of questions about Gorodisce, like the names of neighbors living next to us, as though trying to confirm my story. She said that it was a pity that I came today, so unexpectedly. She said that next time we should set a prearranged time for me to come. She kept asking me to stay awhile longer, to wait for her husband's return. When she went to the kitchen to prepare some tea, I snuck around the sleeping alcove curtain. I saw a picture of a man dressed in a uniform that looked very similar to a German's uniform. Whoever that man is, he must be a collaborator. When she returned, I excused myself, saying that I had to leave right away because I left my daughter alone and must be back home before sunset. I promised to come again in two weeks time to return the books she loaned to me. Benny, I did not like it at all," mother admitted.

I was very relieved that my mother had reached this conclusion and that she would not endanger her life for the pleasure of reading books.

Life at this time, in this part of the forest, was safer than during the previous year when, for most of the time, we led a nomadic life. Here we could stay in our hut permanently, not having to seek safe shelter each night and we had a reasonable supply of food.

Most of the villagers in this area cooperated with the partisans and willingly contributed food to the brigade. During the summer months, the forest offered an abundance of edible plants, mushrooms, and berries, which we collected. We sent some of this bounty to the main camp as our way of helping the fighters. I no longer had any need to sneak over to the fields of nearby villages to steal food.

But the war was still going on and we were not totally safe. We were still in danger from the German airplanes and the Ukrainian pro-Nazi bands that roamed the forest. We had to keep a low profile, stay hidden, and do all we could to survive. At least now we had the hope that survival was possible.

Our health was in better hands as a medical doctor and nurses treated our sick and wounded. We dressed in castoff uniforms that the partisans in the main camp received from the Red Army. Other warm clothes were obtained by raiding German Army barracks and by confiscating clothes from collaborators.

A shortwave radio supplied the partisans with news about the war. The main camp printed a bulletin, which was distributed among the villagers, encouraging them to join the partisans and fight against the hated Nazis, who by this time committed so many atrocities against them. We received those bulletins as well at the family camp and knew what was going on in other parts of Russia and the Ukraine.

As time went on, the news improved each day. Early in 1943, we heard that the German Army was defeated at Stalingrad. Now, as summer was approaching once again, it became obvious that they were retreating. This was the right time to strike them, as often as possible, when they were most vulnerable.

Now, the partisans had a better supply of ammunition and explosives. They were able to derail German supply trains by using these explosives, not needing to use the same method we had employed to derail the first train. The partisans attacked German units in isolated villages and constantly threatened their safety.

I was itching to join the action before it was too late. Finally, at the end of the summer, my father called me aside and said, "Benny, you are needed in the main camp. I was ordered to bring you back with me. I know that this will be very hard on your mother, and I, too, would be happier if you stayed here with her, but there is nothing we can do about it. Go say goodbye to your mother and Sheindale. Prepare yourself to leave."

Father spoke quietly with my mother, telling her about my new orders. I began putting my belongings together in a bundle, and preparing myself for the hard part – saying goodbye to my mother and my little sister, from whom I was separated only for short periods of time since the war began.

When the moment came to actually leave, Sheindale cried and would not let go of my hands. My mother's eyes, too, were full of tears as she hugged me. I heard her murmuring a quiet blessing. I felt sad, but I was proud to be called to arms, to be a fighting man, at last.

10

At Last – A Fighting Man

This was my second visit to the main camp of the Russian partisan brigade. This time I came not as a mere visitor, but as a full-fledged member. As a safety precaution, members of the family camps were discouraged from visiting this site unless they had specific duties to perform.

Father took me around the camp and showed me the various huts designated for specific military functions. The most important one was the commander's office – the headquarters of the brigade. Another important place was the medical hut and another was the kitchen.

Then he showed me the hut where my sister, Dina, lived with a number of other partisan women. All the huts were built from logs and situated underneath old trees, nestling under their branches for protection. The men lived in adjacent huts that were dug into the rich forest soil and covered with branches. The bunkers were warm in the winter, but very hot and airless in the summer. In all, the camp was as secure as could be from enemy attacks.

"We have a number of horses," my father said, "but they are tied down in a camouflaged area, a little way from the main camp. They are our main mode of transportation."

We walked in silence for a few moments and then he said, "Now let's go and meet our platoon leader, Yafim Ivanovitch. He is probably in the headquarters hut. He will give you your orders and instruct you about your duties. You must obey his orders because you are a soldier now, a member of this brigade."

Ivanovitch, a middle-aged sturdily built man, was in the hut, standing in front of a map of the area. I saluted him as smartly as I could, despite my bundle, and said, "Comrade Commandant, Benyamin Davidovitch reporting for duty."

A smile spread over his round face. My father seemed to be proud of my proper military conduct.

"At ease, young comrade, we are not too formal around here." Turning toward my father, he said, "I see that you have a real soldier for a son." Then focusing his attention once again on me, he said in a quiet voice, "There are a number of assignments a young man like you can perform, to help us in our fight against the Nazi enemy of our motherland. Do you know how to shoot?"

"Yes, Comrade Officer, I know how to shoot a rifle and a handgun," I answered. "My father taught me how to use the weapons, but I have not had too many chances to use them against the enemy."

"Your father told me that you took part in actions against the Nazis, and that you are good at gathering information," Ivanovitch said.

"We need someone who can fight, but we also need someone who is bright and can go unnoticed into the villages in the area to gather information about Nazi soldiers and about Ukrainian collaborators. We also need help with distributing news bulletins to the local population. It is important that they all realize that the Russian forces will soon defeat the German Army. We need them to help us in our fight," Ivanovitch added.

He looked at the map for a moment and asked, "Do you know how to ride a horse? Do you know how to drive a wagon?" I nodded my head in confirmation of my ability to do both.

"Very good, very good," the commander said. He seemed pleased with my expertise. "We might send you to some outlying villages to carry out certain orders. You will be informed about that at the proper time."

Once again, he stopped talking and looked at the charts on his makeshift desk.

Then the commander continued, "Right now we need someone bright and agile, able to climb up a tree and serve as an airplane spotter. We need advance warning of approaching Nazi airplanes. This is very important for the safety of the camp. The spotter must be very alert, and have keen eyesight and hearing, in order to carry out this assignment in the best possible way. Do you think that you can do this?"

I was looking forward to be sent right away to some dangerous mission where I could prove myself a brave and experienced partisan. So I was a little disappointed that my first duty seemed so unimportant, but I answered without any hesitation, "Yes Comrade Ivanovitch, I will obey your command and fulfill it to the best of my ability."

"That is all for today, young man. Your father will help you to settle in your hut and acquaint you with the safety regulations of this camp. Come back to headquarters tomorrow morning and I will give you your orders," he said and indicated that we were dismissed.

I asked the one question that was uppermost in my mind. "Are there any other boys my age in this camp?"

"No, my boy, most of the men in this camp are older than you," he answered. I was really sorry to hear this, because I had hoped to meet other boys in this camp and make friends with them. It had been a long time since I last talked or spent time with someone my age. But this could not be helped.

Father took me to his hut and introduced me to his hutmates who were busy cleaning their rifles or mending their clothes or just laying on their bunks. They welcomed me warmly.

The next morning, bright and early, I went to the headquarters hut. Ivanovitch was there with another man, whom he introduced to me as Oleg, my platoon commander. Oleg, a blond, blue-eyed man of Polish descent, informed me that my first duty was to learn how to become a good airplane spotter. He showed me a strange gadget, a square box enclosed in a leather cover, with a handle sticking out from one side, and a black tube with two bulbs at both ends, resting on a cradle.

"This is a field telephone. Do you know how to use it?" he asked. I was a bit embarrassed at my ignorance, but admitted that I did not.

"Well, not to worry. I will show you. There is a similar field telephone kept permanently on the tree platform where you will be stationed. That telephone is connected by wire to this hut. We use the telephone to pass information to the duty officer.

Here's how the telephone works. Turn this handle a few times, lift the handset from the cradle and talk clearly and slowly into it." He demonstrated how to turn the handle, how to hold the telephone and speak clearly into the mouthpiece. He made me practice using the field telephone until he was sure that I knew what I was doing. Then he said, "Go to the kitchen and get some food and a canteen of water. Tell them that this is an order. Also, bring along a warm coat."

I did as I was told. I got food and water from the kitchen and picked up a warm coat from my hut, where I told my father what I was ordered to do. Then I went back to the headquarters where Oleg was waiting. We walked along one of those half-hidden trails for what seemed a long time. Finally we stopped next to a tall tree with a thick trunk, which had some notches cut into it.

"This is your post," Oleg said. "Take these binoculars with you and climb up the tree until you reach the small platform at the top. You will see the field telephone up there and a basket tied to a cord. Lower the basket to me and I will send up your food and your coat. Conceal yourself among the branches, and keep a sharp lookout for approaching airplanes. Any plane you will see is an enemy plane. Russian planes do not fly in these parts during the day.

If you spot a plane, use the phone the way I showed you to

inform the command center at headquarters. Watch the forest as well. If you spot any suspicious movement on the ground – call headquarters. Don't hesitate to call. You need to understand, it is better to call and alert us, than to miss something suspicious." I nodded.

"Now, climb up and get settled on the platform. Here are your binoculars. I will come at sundown to take you back to the camp."

Without saying another word, I climbed up the notches on the trunk, and then continued to climb higher and higher, from one branch to another, until I reached the platform.

"Comrade Oleg," I called out, "I am on the platform."

I saw the basket and lowered it to him. He put my provisions into it. I drew it back up. He turned to leave, but stopped and asked, "Do you have your gun and ammunition?"

"Yes, Comrade Oleg, I don't go anywhere without my gun!" I answered with pride.

I settled on the platform, arranging the field telephone, the water and food within easy reach. Sitting on the hard wooden planks with nothing to do, trying not to move too much was not easy for me. If I had any choice in the matter, I wouldn't have chosen to be a plane-spotter. But orders are orders. If I wanted to be accepted as a full-fledged partisan, I had to obey them.

It was very boring. Time hardly seemed to go by. In the back of my mind, I hoped that enemy planes would come flying our way, searching for us. I imagined how I would alert the camp and save the people in it. I could hear in my mind the praises heaped on me for this heroic deed. But as a matter of fact, nothing happened that day, or any other day. I kept wishing that I had a book to read, or something to do to make the time pass faster. No such luck. All I could do was think about my life at home, about my friends, about the games we used to play. Oh, how good it was then, and now it was all gone.

As the long, long day progressed, it got colder and I was glad that I had a warm coat to wear. I had to fight the urge to fall asleep. Being asleep while on duty would have ended my career as a partisan once and for all. This was not a job for me, I thought, whether important or not. This was a job for someone who could sit patiently on his behind for many hours. I needed action! By the time Oleg came for me, I was very cold and bored to death.

Despite these feelings, I returned to the tree for the next few days. Fall was upon us and it rained almost daily. The sky was overcast with dark rain-laden clouds. Oleg told me that I did not have to go to the observation post until the weather cleared. I hoped that I would not need to do this even after the rain stopped and that I would be assigned to other duties. Meanwhile, I was sent, temporarily, to help take care of the horses. This was more to my liking because I loved horses. Still, I wished to be assigned to some new duties, where I would take part in the action.

During this time our fight against the enemy was carried out relentlessly. The men in our camp kept coming and going. Some disappeared for a few days and returned tired and dirty. At times, I saw them carrying a wounded comrade to the medical hut for treatment.

The ways in which the returning men reacted to their recent battle experiences differed from man to man. Some men clammed up, hardly greeting those who stayed behind. They would fall asleep immediately, right after they finished eating their meager meal. Others seemed full of energy. Restless, they would tell me in great detail about the battle, as though sharing their experiences made it easier for them to relax. I would listen eagerly to their stories.

I did not know where they went or where they fought, but how I wanted to go with them, how I wanted to take an active part in a battle.

My father went along on some of these sorties. Other times he went with one or two men to scout out the area. At such times, I would wait anxiously for his return. My father was among the quiet ones. I never heard from him what he and his unit did when they were sent to fight.

In the main camp, there was a certain military routine that had to be adhered to. Between battles, the men stood guard, cleaned their rifles, mended their clothes, trimmed their hair and rested. Those who had families in the family camp were allowed to visit them. We went to visit my mother and young sister whenever we could.

All this time, Dina lived in the main camp, in a hut assigned to women partisans. Two other women from our original group lived in the same hut with her. She, too, felt that she would be much better able to contribute to the war against the Nazis as part of a partisan combat unit. But in reality, only a few women were allowed to take part in the battles. Most were assigned to duties in the camp, serving as nurses and cooks.

Being almost a high-school graduate, Dina was assigned to do clerical work. She typed the news bulletins on the precious typewriter kept in the headquarters hut and helped the commander whenever official letters had to be typed and sent to the Russian Army command.

Dina had the opportunity to learn to use the typewriter after our original group "liberated" the typewriter from the municipal office in Malinsk.

There were very few typewriters in our area, so it was a great honor to be allowed to use such a wonderful machine. Seeing my sister typing on it as part of her daily duties made me very proud of her, even though I never told her.

But the way she treated me was at times very annoying. Being the older sister, she felt that she had to care for me as though she were my mother. She would try to hug me right in front of the other men.

"Benny," she would say, "Have you already eaten today?"

"Yes I ate." I would grumble.

"Benny, did you wash today? Come to my hut. I have a clean shirt for you.

"Benny, can I help you with something?" She always asked in the concerned way of an older sister. She was ready and willing to help.

"I don't need anything, I can take care of myself," I answered, hoping that nobody would hear this conversation.

This was a bit embarrassing. After all, I wasn't a little boy anymore. I could take care of myself and even of her. Hadn't I proven it in the past?

Finally, my turn for action came. That evening, I was told to present myself at the headquarters the next morning.

Right after sunup, my father shook my shoulder and said, "Benny it's time to get up." Half asleep, I washed my face in icy cold water. This really woke me up. I went to the headquarters hut where Oleg was already waiting for me.

"We need to deliver these news bulletins to Balasivka, which is located some distance from here. It is important to let the villagers know what is happening in Russia. It is important that they do their best to hinder the Nazis in this war," Oleg told me.

"We have information that there are a number of collaborators in this village who are helping the Nazis. This bulletin urges them to refrain from helping the enemy, or fear death.

"We, at headquarters, decided that the best way to bring this message to the villagers would be for you to slip into the village and deliver these leaflets. You will go to the house of one of the villagers, a man who is loyal to us. He will be able to distribute them secretly among his neighbors. A stranger doing this might be easily spotted by one of the collaborators and arrested."

I nodded my head, taking in his words, making instant plans on how to best carry out my orders. But Oleg had a lot more to say.

"In order to ensure your safety, you will go to the village dressed as a girl. It is market day in Balasivka, so no one will pay attention to a girl walking about and looking at the goods." A smile appeared on his face, and disappeared just as fast when he saw my reaction. "Benny, I promise you that in this disguise you will be safe. I will make arrangements for you to be driven to the village in a wagon because it is too far to walk and make it in time."

"Do I really have to dress as a girl?" I asked again, trying to avert this order.

"Yes, you must. You have no choice in this matter. It is for your own protection. What you are about to do is very dangerous. If you are caught with these leaflets in your possession, you will be shot on the spot," Oleg answered.

"The Nazis and their friends do not tolerate our spreading news of Russian success among the population. They want to keep the villagers ignorant, scared and obedient, especially now, when the Nazis have been defeated in Stalingrad and are in retreat. Shooting a partisan is the Nazi way of intimidating and scaring the villagers, deterring them from helping us. Dressed as a girl, you will have a better chance of going unnoticed. It will be safer for you and safer for the man you have to meet."

Oleg turned toward Dina, who walked into the hut as though on cue. "Your sister will help you dress and give you the leaflets to take with you. She will also tell you how to make contact with our man. Remember, don't talk to the wagon driver about your mission. The wagon driver has additional duties to perform, but that is his business, and none of yours. The less you know about each other's assignments, the better. When you are done, go back to where you were dropped off. The wagon will be there, waiting for you. Good luck, comrade!" He shook my hand and walked away.

My sister proceeded to dress me as a girl. I have no idea from where she got the long skirt, the embroidered blouse, the coat, and the colorful kerchief.

"Here," she said as she handed over the clothes. "Take off your pants and put these on, but leave your boots on. After all, men, boys, and girls wear these same type of boots."

I knew that I had to do as I was told, because there was no other person who could replace me on this assignment.

After I had dressed in the skirt and blouse, my sister tied the kerchief on my head. She looked at me and started to giggle, but she suppressed the laugh. She looked at me with a critical expression on her face. "Yes. No... I don't know... Something is missing," she muttered to herself. "Yes, something is missing... Hair... You don't have enough hair to pass as a girl," she exclaimed. And then my sister did something, which left me speechless. She took a knife and chopped off her own two braids.

"What are you doing? You cut off your braids! Oh, wait until mother sees you!" I cried out.

Dina was a very beautiful girl, with high cheekbones, sparkling hazel eyes, an up-tilted nose and full lips with long, long braids hanging down to her waist. Her long braids enhanced her beauty and she was very proud of them. She wore them as a crown on top of her head, or as buns over her ears, or crisscrossed in the back and tied with a ribbon. At times she just let them hang on her chest like two thick brown ropes. Even in the worst of times in the ghetto and in the forest, she would groom her long brown hair, complaining all the time how hard it was to comb. I always thought that she looked like a princess from biblical times.

How could she have cut off those braids, her pride and joy?

Dina did not pay attention to my reaction and proceeded to remove the kerchief from my head, pin her braids to my own hair while saying, "I have been wanting to do this for a long time now. This long hair is a real nuisance here in the camp. I am better off without the braids. Maybe now they will consider me fit to join a real fighting unit." She fussed with me for a few more minutes until she was satisfied with my looks. "Anyway, I did this for a good cause," she said, as though in consolation for a seemingly hasty act.

"Now we have to make up a cover story for you. First, we have to give you a name, and teach you to act like a girl," she said. "You must remember everything, exactly as we have practiced, and stick to it when asked any questions," she added.

"Now, let's see... You are Marinka Goluboy. You live in the village..." She looked at the map, pointed at a name. "You are from Malushka, and you have come with your father to buy some supplies. Your father went to feed the oxen, and told you that you could look around at the merchandise in the stalls. He said that he would stop for a drink in the pub. Yes, this is a good cover story." She was very satisfied with her clever invention.

She made me repeat my new name, and the reasons for my being there on my own until I knew them by heart.

"Good. Now that you know your name and cover story you must learn to act like a girl. Walk toward me, slowly. Slowly. Take small steps. Remember you are a girl, not a tomboy. Don't walk or behave like one. If you feel that you are in danger, start crying – and keep on crying. Other villagers might take pity on a girl crying and help her." Again and again, she made me practice walking like a girl, until she was satisfied. Then she gave me a basket filled with apples. The leaflets were hidden under the apples.

"Here are your instructions. You are to go to the house belonging to a farmer named Stepan. The house is located in an alley on the left side of the market square. It is the last house in the alley. The house has green shutters. Precisely at noon, a woman will be sitting outside the door, holding a baby in her arms. Go to her and ask her if she wants to buy your red apples, which you picked in the morning. She will answer that she needs apples to bake a cake for her mother-in-law who is coming to visit. This is the secret code. Memorize it well. Only when you are sure that the right words were spoken, will you know that you are at the right house. She will ask you to go to the kitchen and put the apples on the table because she is busy with the baby. Leave the apples on the table, but hide the bulletins in the pile of wood next to the oven. Then leave the house and go back to the outskirts of the village to meet the wagon driver. Remember, no heroics. Leave the leaflets, and come back."

I wondered how my sister knew all these details, but refrained from asking too many questions, and did what I was told. We had little time to waste. I was in a hurry to learn my part and go to meet the wagon.

Dina gave me a fast hug and then walked with me toward the waiting wagon. Some partisans were looking at us. Did they look at my sister who had cut her braids, or did they look at the Ukrainian girl who walked beside her? I did not know. Maybe they were used to seeing strange sights and had learned to ignore them.

The wagon was hitched to two oxen. The drive to the village was slow and uneventful. Still, it was better than having to walk the whole distance. At the outskirts of the village, we arranged a meeting place, and the driver turned back. He had things to do and the wagon had to stay safely hidden in the forest until I came back. He told me that on the way back from the village he was ordered to pick up some supplies from a farmer who lived up the road, but my assignment came first.

I walked toward the market square, telling myself to walk slowly, to walk like a girl, because my life depended on it. Once more, I was confronted with the fact that my assignment was really not too dangerous, that all I had to do was deliver my basket and return. No one would give me a medal of heroism for doing this.

The market was busy with farmers coming and going, buying and selling goods. A Ukrainian policeman, dressed in a uniform similar to the German uniforms, patrolled the stalls and stopped to talk to some of the men.

Women with babushkas on their heads stood at the stalls, selling their wares. The men seemed to drift toward the pub, which was crowded and noisy. Young children ran about shouting at the top of their voices. Market day was a good excuse for them not to attend school.

As I had a little time to spare before the meeting, I walked slowly from stall to stall looking at the merchandise, trying to blend in, not wanting to draw any attention to myself. Above all, I kept out of the way of the policeman.

I was so busy acting like a girl, that I did not pay attention to what was right in front of me. I bumped into a young boy of fifteen or sixteen. He caught me by my arm. "Hey, watch out! Where are you going my pretty girl?" he asked me in a jeering voice. I tried to shake off his hand, bent my head and lowered my eyes, just like a bashful girl would do, but the boy would not let go of my arm. Four more boys, evidently his friends, joined us and kept making funny remarks about me and about him and laughed at their own cleverness. I realized that I did not bump into him, but that he bumped into me, probably on a dare from his friends.

"Come, come, look at me. Don't be ashamed! What's your

name?" he asked. "Marinka," I mumbled, while in my mind I was trying to figure out the best way to get rid of these boys without attracting too much attention to myself. I realized that as long as I had the bulletins in my basket, I was in great danger. It was ironic. Here I was trying to escape notice by the police and instead these young bullies were threatening me.

"Come with us, Marinka," continuing to talk, all the while holding my arm. "We will buy you a ribbon for your pretty braids, and you will show us your pretty..." Before he had a chance to finish his sentence, he let go of my arm. I looked up. A man dressed in a long black robe was shaking his fist at the boy. The boy turned around and escaped. His buddies ran after him.

"Don't mind these bullies," the black-robed man said to me in a kind voice. "I will keep my eyes on those guys. They will not bother you again, my girl. They know better than to disobey a priest. Surely you are not alone here. Where are your parents? I will take you to them."

Oh no, I thought, out of the frying pan into the fire. This was really turning out to be a bad day for me. It was a well known fact that the Ukrainian priests were collaborating with the Nazis. They had two good reasons for doing so. They hated the Russians who were opposed to religion and disbanded the Church. They helped the Nazis because they hated the Jews. I knew that I must get rid of my new protector, for my own safety and for the safety of my mission. What could I do?

Then I remembered my sister's advice. Cry! Cry!

I started crying and wailing loudly, "I am afraid, Holy Father. These boys were mean to me. I am here with my father, but he went to feed the oxen in back of the pub. He told me to wait for him at the stall selling pots and pans right by the pub. Then he went into the pub to have a drink. I waited and waited. Then I went to look at other stalls, and got lost. Please take me back to the pub. I can't go inside. Could you go in there and find him? I will wait for him just where he told me to wait. He will be very angry with me if he learns that I did not wait for him. He will punish me. Please, Holy Father, look for him in the pub. Tell him to come and get me. His name is Ivan

Antonovitch from the village of Malushka."

I grabbed his hand and kissed it, all the time I keeping my head bent, crying.

The priest must have had a soft heart or else he did not like to hear a girl crying. He asked me to stop crying and follow him. He took me to the vicinity of the pub.

"There. There. This is where I am to wait for my father." I pointed to a nearby stall selling pots and pans. "He must still be in the pub. Please get him. I will wait here."

The kindly priest patted my head, told me to stay put and walked toward the pub. As soon as he walked inside, I sauntered to the other side of the stall, then started walking as fast as I could in the opposite direction, into a small alley, which led out of the market square.

I was praying very hard for my luck to change, and that I would find the house where I was supposed to leave the news bulletins. I knew that I could not go back to the market square. Too many people might be looking for me, asking questions.

When the church bells started ringing, I was so startled by the sudden noise that I almost jumped into the air. I started to count: two, three... ten, eleven, twelve. It was noon, time to go to find the house and deliver the leaflets. I kept walking in the alley, hoping that this was the right direction.

Indeed my luck had turned. This was the alley I was supposed to follow. The last house had green shutters. A young woman holding a baby was sitting in front of the house. I approached the woman and asked her if she would buy my red apples, which I had picked early this very morning. The woman answered me with the correct code and told me to go and put the apples in the kitchen. Before going into the house I looked at her. Could I trust her? Would she be able to help me?

"I am in danger," I said in a hushed voice. "I can't go back to the market square, but I do not know how to get to the forest from here. Please help me." She stood up. Her face registered fear and some anger. If I was in danger, I might bring the same danger upon her and her family. For a moment she hesitated, then she said in a gruff voice, "Go inside – fast!"

Inside the house, I said "Don't worry, it was not the policeman, just some boys who were teasing me, and the priest who helped me and went to find my father. He might be looking for me."

The woman seemed relieved. She asked me for the leaflets, which I gladly gave her. She took them to the other room. Then, she put a shawl over her head and shoulders, picked up the sleeping baby, and said, "I am going to visit my friend. Her house is closest to the forest. I will be going through the back path. It's a shortcut to her house. Go out now, wait for me to leave the house, and follow me at a distance. After I enter my friend's house, go along the path. It will bring you to the road that leads out of the village." She made the sign of a cross over my head. "Good luck. May God watch over you."

I followed her instructions and finally reached the forest. Then I took another path, which took me to the main road. From there I continued to the prearranged meeting place. The wagon driver was already there, waiting for me. We walked some more, turned into the forest, and there was the wagon with the oxen, munching on some straw. We climbed onto the wagon and were on our way. We made the pre-planned stop at the farmer's house, loaded the wagon with some bales of straw and a few sacks of feed for the horses and went back to the camp.

For once I was very glad that this mission had come to an end. I hoped that there would be no more need to send me anywhere dressed as a girl. Obviously, girls were in a lot more danger than could be imagined, and not only from the Nazis.

My sister was happy to see me. While changing my clothes, I told her about my adventures as a girl. She laughed heartily upon hearing my story. I made her promise not to tell anyone in the camp about it.

The next time we went to visit the family camp, my mother was very surprised about my sister's short haircut. She knew how much Dina loved her long braids. Sheindale kept looking at Dina and touching her short hair as though trying to make the hair grow into long braids once again.

To distract my mother and little sister, Dina told them about my adventure as a girl, despite my protests. They all had a good laugh, and my father who joined us later, laughed as well. I did not think it was very funny, but if they could have a good laugh, even at my expense, so be it. After all, we really had very little to laugh about.

11

The Death Of My Sister

O nce more, a magnificent fall came to the forest. This was our second fall here. Our situation had changed for the better in many ways. We were now in a part of the Ukraine, although still under German occupation, which was under the control of the Russian partisans. They were the masters of the dense forest and the bog. We could stay in our camps without the need to wander from place to place to find safety. We were physically and emotionally stronger after having survived more than a year in the forest. We learned how to survive under the harshest conditions, how to turn the forest into a friend and to take advantage of what it had to offer us. We had enough rifles, machine guns, grenades and explosives to make our battles with the Nazis more successful. We had enough food to sustain us, enough clothes to keep us warm, and best of all, now we had the hope that we would survive, that the enemy would be defeated and we would be liberated.

I was, by now, a full-fledged member of the partisan brigade in the main camp. I even took part in a few battles, punishment raids against collaborators, as well as missions against German troops and convoys. On the occasions that I could join in the actual fighting, I had a chance to shoot my rifle at passing convoys of German trucks. It was very exciting and a bit scary. Did I kill anyone? I honestly did not know. I tried my best to aim well and hit the enemy. On such occasions, after we were safely in the camp, the officer in charge of the unit would slap my back, and say "So, you like to fight, eh?" I would nod my head and answer "Yes, comrade."

We were lucky. We sustained very few casualties that fall, but the sight of a dead or a wounded partisan still affected us strongly. The whole camp grieved for the dead and hoped that the wounded would recover. The most seriously injured were taken by airplanes to hospitals in the unoccupied part of Russia.

Many times I joined small partisan units who were sent to obtain food. I had some experience in doing that. When I took no part in the action against the enemy, I was assigned to stand guard at the main camp while the other men fought. At times, I was ordered to take care of the horses, which were tied under the cover of dense interwoven branches in a copse of trees close to the main camp.

As winter was approaching once again, our commanders told us that it would be harder for us to continue to carry out ambushes against our enemies because the Germans traveled much less during the cold snowy months. We had to take the initiative and carry the fight to them. We would go to their strongholds, losing the element of surprise, and fight against an entrenched defense. This was a more dangerous type of battle and the price in partisan lives would be much higher. But not one of us ever thought of not fighting, of leaving the enemy alone. It was our duty as partisans to harass the enemy, to make his life harder and more dangerous. This was our way of doing our share for the war effort and helping the Russian Army which, at that time, was winning many battles and liberating more and more of occupied Russia, coming steadily closer to this part of the Ukraine.

My father, Dina, and I went to visit my mother and Sheindale as often as possible, always bringing them food. Being active fighting partisans, we were entitled to better and more generous rations, so we were always able to save something special for them to eat.

Toward the end of January, when father and I arrived at the family camp, mother told us that Sheindale was sick. She had a high fever and was laying on the cot, covered with many layers of clothes and blankets. Her small body kept shaking with cold and her usually happy smile, which greeted us every time we came, was gone. Mother was very worried.

My father left quickly to find the doctor from the main camp. He came and examined my little sister. "I believe she has scarlet fever," he said. "There is little I can do for her, but I can tell you this much. If she is to survive this illness, she needs a warm house and better food. Given these, the sickness will run its course, and she will recover."

"We must do something. It is so cold and damp here, and we have no milk for the little one," my mother kept repeating tearfully.

Then my father said, "I will go and ask my friend Kerylo, a farmer in a nearby small village, Berezniki, to take you and Sheindale into his house to give her a better chance for recovery. In his house you will have a warm shelter and fresh milk for Sheindale."

"Yes, that is a good idea," mother said. "I hope that he will agree. Hurry. Go and find out."

We hoped that hiding in the village would not be too dangerous for everyone concerned, especially now, when the Germans rarely came to this area in the middle of the winter.

Father left, and when he returned, he brought with him a small sled. "Kerylo, a good man, has agreed to hide you in his house and take care of you until she gets well," he said bringing a smile to my mother's worried face. That same afternoon, Sheindale, well bundled against the cold, was placed on the sled. Then we walked to the village. Father and I took turns pulling the sled over the deep snow.

It was turning dark when we finally reached the outskirts of the village. We waited a bit longer beneath the trees, and then, under the cover of darkness, we walked to Kerylo's house, hoping no one had seen us. Kerylo, his wife Toniya, and daughter welcomed us. They made a bed for Sheindale right on the sleeping bench next to the stove, the warmest place in the house. They served us some food and asked my father and me to stay awhile and warm up, before starting back on our cold walk to the partisan camp.

One more member of the family made us feel welcome as well – a large, beautiful dog, with smart eyes and a shiny black coat. The dog approached us and smelled us. Once he confirmed that we were friends, he licked my hand as he wagged his tail.

I petted him and pulled him close to me while I scratched behind his ears. "Good dog, you are a good dog," I whispered in his ear. He reminded me very much of Rex, my own dog, whom I missed.

After seeing that my mother and Sheindale were settled in comfortably, we thanked Kerylo and Toniya and took our leave. We promised my mother that we would come back in two day's time to see how Sheindale was doing.

The walk back was indeed long and cold. In the camp, Dina was waiting for us, very concerned about Sheindale's health.

"Don't worry. Your mother and sister are fine. They will be well taken care of, and soon Sheindale will get well. We will go and visit them in a couple of days," father said.

"I will come with you," Dina stated, leaving no room for argument.

We were sure that no one had seen us coming and leaving Kerylo's house, but as it turned out, we were wrong, and we paid dearly for this mistake.

We were all aware that even this late in the war, the Nazis still kept paying a reward to anyone who informed against their neighbors who hid Jewish survivors or handed over Jewish survivors to the Ukrainian police. The going price for a Jewish life was still a kilo salt, two kilos sugar and a small sum of money. The reward for a Jewish partisan was double that!

Evidently someone who had no problem informing the

Nazis about refugees hiding in the village, had seen us entering Kerylo's house and notified the Germans. Who that person was, we never found out. Unbeknownst to us, the Nazis occupied Kerylo's house and took my mother, Sheindale, Kerylo, and his family captive, making it impossible for them to warn us about the danger. They left three soldiers in the house, ready to ambush us. Two days later, when we came to visit my mother and little sister, we walked right into the trap.

As the three of us entered the house, one of the Germans said, "Halt! Raise your hands! Don't move!"

As I was behind my father and Dina, I instinctively backed out of the door, and ran as fast as I could toward the forest. Dina followed me. My father did not run. As he told me later, he just could not leave my mother and Sheindale to a fate worse than death. He stood in the kitchen with his hands in the air, at the mercy of the enemy. Panic and confusion seemed to affect my mother, who stood closest to the bed where the unconscious Sheindale was laying, unable to move. Two German soldiers stood pointing their rifles at her and at my father. Another Nazi soldier was pointing his rifle at Kerylo, Toniya, and their daughter.

"I was sure that Sheindale was dead. So I concentrated on saving your mother," he told me. "I shouted in Russian, 'Mania, at my sign, jump through the window next to you and run to the forest. I will get out through the other window. Now! Run! Run!'"

Without thinking, my dazed mother obeyed his order and launched herself through the window nearest to her. Father ran toward the other window, set in the opposite wall, and tried to jump through it. The German soldier dropped his rifle and caught the tail of his long coat and held onto it, all the while shouting, "Halt! Halt!"

In all this confusion, the farmer's dog, excited by the noise and the sudden movements, jumped on the soldier who was holding onto my father's coat, and bit him in the leg. The soldier let out a loud scream and let go of the coat. At last my father was free to make his escape. The other soldiers, momentarily stunned by the dog's attack and father's escape, pointed their rifles at the two broken windows through which my parents escaped and started shooting at the escapees.

All this time, which actually lasted only a few minutes, Dina and I did not know what was happening. From behind the tree where we were crouching, we could hear the sound of barking and the rifle fire. Dina jumped up, very agitated.

"Stay here," she said in a tight voice. "I must go and see what happened to mother and father."

"Don't go, don't go," I warned, but she did not pay attention to me. She ran swiftly toward the house, not thinking about taking any precautions, not thinking about her own safety. The German soldiers kept shooting. I saw her stumble and fall, her hands clutching her head. She did not move.

"Dina, Dina," I cried. As I got up from my crouched position, I ran toward her. In my heart I knew that she was dead. I knew that I could not help her. Subconsciously, I perceived that if I ran to where she fell, so much closer to the house, I, too, would be killed. My self-preservation instinct intervened, and made me stop. I retreated back into the forest. I believed that Sheindale was also dead by now, killed by the same Nazi murderers. Continuing along the same line of thought, I reasoned that if my father or mother survived, they would need at least one of their children at their side.

I turned away from the terrible scene, leaving behind me the house of death and escaped to the forest, tears of anger and grief running down my cheeks. I don't recall how long I was running. I seemed to be lost, but I kept on running and running, until finally I was stopped by one of the guards posted around the main camp. He recognized me and took me to the camp headquarters where I reported what had happened to my family.

"My sisters are dead," I told the officer on duty, "but maybe my parents survived. We must go there and find out what happened to them." Tears kept running down my face. I just could not stop them. The officer tried to console me. "Hold on Benny. In the morning we will send a scouting party. We will find your parents," he promised me.

"Please Comrade, let me go with them. Maybe I can help my parents." I kept begging him for permission to go with the scouting party. He hesitated, but when he saw my tear-streaked face, he agreed to let me go.

That night was the longest night in my whole life. Not knowing what had happened to my beloved family was terrible. I was sure that they were all dead, or even worse, held captive by the Nazis. I kept blaming myself for running away, for not trying to find them. I felt guilty for having survived while my beloved family perished. I laid on my cot in our hut, crying, waiting for the coming of dawn, praying for a miracle. The kind words of my hut-mates did not quell my anguish or diminish my feelings of guilt.

In the morning, a group of men, including Leibl, who was a member of our original group and a dear friend of my father's, and Yonah, Dina's friend, met at the headquarters. Oleg was put in charge of our small unit.

"We are going to walk toward the village staying hidden as long as possible. We will try to find out what the situation is over there. If the German soldiers are still inside the house, we can't do anything. If they are gone, we will try to find out what happened to your family," he said. "Remember, Benny, this is a scouting party. We are not strong enough to engage the enemy in a fight. Such an action would endanger us all, including your family. These are my orders. You must obey them, no matter what."

I knew that his words made sense, but in my heart I also knew that for me there was no room for sensible behavior. I would try to find out what happened to my parents and sisters, or die in the attempt and join my family in death.

Our scouting party set out toward the village. I walked as if in a nightmare that kept repeating itself. Then suddenly two white ghosts, one of them carrying a bundle, appeared in front of us. I heard my father's voice saying, "Benny, Benny, thank God, you are safe." He hugged me and then my mother hugged me, and a big stone seemed to roll off my heart. I realized that both my parents were alive, and so was little Sheindale, whom they carried, all bundled up against the cold.

"Tell me what happened," I asked, torn between happiness at seeing them alive and between fear of hearing the confirmation of what I already knew – that Dina was dead.

"Later son, later. First we must go back to the camp," father said. "We need to find shelter for your mother and your little sister."

We hurried back to the main camp. My father took my mother, who appeared to be dazed, and Sheindale who seemed to be better, to the infirmary. The doctor was summoned to help them while Leibl ran to the kitchen to obtain hot tea and some food for them. Yonah stood in the corner, tears running down his face, unable to hide his feelings. Dina and Yonah had become very close friends. On many occasions, I saw them sitting together on a log, talking quietly, totally absorbed in each other. Dina's death was very hard for him, too.

Father did not want any food. "We have no time," he said. "We must go and help Kerylo. He and his family are being held prisoner in the policeman's house. We must set them free and bring them here. I am going to headquarters to obtain permission from the brigade commander to rescue these good people." He was like a man possessed, unable to find rest for his troubled soul. He turned and walked swiftly toward headquarters. When he returned, he told us that permission was given to rescue Kerylo and his family.

My father was put in charge of a large unit of well-armed men. I was allowed to join them. Because time was of the essence, we had permission to ride horses to our destination. We proceeded at a fast trot toward the village.

The members of our unit were determined to do their best to save this man and his family who had helped us in our time of need, and now were doomed to pay with their own lives for their kindness.

When we reached the village, luck was with us. The German soldiers had already left. It turned out that they were needed urgently at their camp. They were quite sure that no one in the village would dare help Kerylo and his family. They could not have known that help would come from another source – from the partisans in the forest. The local policeman was ordered to transfer the prisoners to a nearby shtetl where they would be hung in the market square. Hanging was the usual punishment for those who disobeyed the Nazis.

Our unit had other plans in mind. It was midday when we entered the village. We walked boldly toward the policeman's house and knocked on the door. When it was opened, my father pointed a gun into the policeman's face and demanded the release of the prisoners. The policeman pointed at the three figures sitting on the kitchen floor, their hands bound behind them. He seemed only too happy to comply. After all, these were his neighbors, and he did not want to see them die.

He caught my father's hand and said, "Please comrade partisan, please, shoot a few rounds of ammunition into the room, break the door, tie my hands and feet, and hit me. Make it look as though I put up a fight, otherwise the Germans will kill me." His words made sense to us. He had to show that he did not cooperate willingly with the partisans and let his prisoners go.

We did as he asked, and the policeman promised that in the future, he would help the partisans as much as he could, without endangering his own family. As a punishment for his long-standing collaboration with the Nazis, we confiscated all the food in the house that we could carry, some warm clothes and warm blankets, which we gave to Kerylo, Toniya, and their daughter. They knew that they could not go back to their house as long as the Germans occupied the area. We turned back toward our camp, Kerylo and his family riding on horseback behind three of our men. Kerylo said to my father, his eyes full of tears, "Believe me Pan Hershko, I don't know who informed the German's about us. I swear to you on the life of my own daughter that I will find the man who destroyed my life, and was responsible for the death of your daughter. I will avenge her death."

On the ride back to camp, father told me what happened inside the house. It was hard for him to speak, but he described in full detail what happened. He told me about the dog that bit the German soldier and enabled him to escape. "That wonderful dog saved my life," father kept saying again and again. "What a miracle. If only he could have saved our Dina. It was lucky that the German soldiers did not dare to follow us into the forest. This saved us."

He told me that he met my mother, who did not run too far into the forest. They did not know what happened to the rest of us so they decided to wait until dawn and try to find out.

He described how he covered my mother with his coat, dug a shelter for the two of them under the snow, and waited for dawn, all the time worrying about what happened to Dina and me. He was also convinced that Sheindale was dead, but did not have the courage to say so. He hoped that we had managed to escape before the shooting started and were safe, hiding just like them in the forest.

At first light, father left my mother in the hiding place and walked stealthily toward the house in an attempt to find out what happened. As he approached the house, a man who was hiding behind a bush stopped him.

"Are you the man who ran away from Kerylo's house last night?" he asked. Father realized that he was in no danger from this man, and shook his head, unable to talk.

"Don't go back to the house. It is not safe. The Germans left in the early morning hours, but they might have left some collaborator on the lookout for you. I live in the house next to Kerylo. When we heard the shots, we did not dare go out to see what was happening," the man continued. "These days it is not safe to stick your nose into other people's troubles. But our neighbor is a relative of my wife's. We watched from behind the shutters of our house and waited. When the Germans left, they took Kerylo and his family with them. After awhile, I went to the house to see what happened."

He sighed, crossed himself and continued talking, "I found Kerylo's dog shot to death, all the furniture broken and all the food gone from the larder. As I stood outside the door, I heard a soft whimper coming from the pile of snow. I went to see what it was, and I found a little girl lying in the snow, cold as a stone, yet still alive. I think that the accursed Nazis did not want to waste a bullet on her. They just threw her out into the snow, to die in the cold, poor little thing. I picked her up and ran back to my house. On the way, I stumbled upon the body of a young woman. I could do nothing for her. I saw that she was shot through the head. She must have died instantly. Was she related to you?" he asked.

My father was unable to answer, but an anguished sob escaped from his clenched lips. He just shook his head. "My daughter," he murmured finally.

"I knew you would come back," the man said. "I waited here for you, to warn you. I have the little girl in my house. She is fine. My wife said that the cold snow took away her fever. Wait here. It is too dangerous to go into the village. I will bring her to you. And I swear on all the saints, that I will bury your daughter in the forest, and mark her grave with a cross."

At last father was able to talk. "Thank you, good man, thank you. Bury my daughter in the forest, but don't mark her grave with a cross because we are Jewish. Please, mark the grave with a stone to remember where you buried her. When this war ends, I will come for her body. Go now and bring my little girl to me. I will wait here for you. Thank you again for your kindness. God will reward you for your good deeds."

Just before the man turned to go, father asked him, "Did the Germans take your neighbors with them or are they still being held in the village?"

"They are being held in the policeman's house," the man answered.

Then he turned and walked toward his house. After a short time, the man came back and handed over the sleeping child to my father.

My father thanked the man again and again and then he walked back to where my mother was hiding. His heart was full of sorrow, yet he knew that he must break the terrible news to my mother. He must tell her about the death of her beloved Dina. His only consolation was that at least he was bringing back to her their younger daughter, alive, and seemingly much better.

"I was worried about you, Benny," he said, "but I knew that given half a chance, you would make it to safety and then come to help us. I was right. That is exactly what you did." His words soothed my own troubled soul, taking away some of the guilt that I felt.

Back in the family camp, we had to face my mother's grief. She was destroyed by sorrow. She seemed to have lost her will to live. Even little Sheindale, who was getting better, but was still very weak and who needed her, was unable to rouse her from her deep agony. It was as though the death of my older sister brought back the pain that she felt after the deaths of our family in the ghetto, only much more so.

Everyone in the main camp grieved for my sister. Surrounded by their sympathy, we too, my father and I, could cry for her. After having survived more than two years in the forest, her luck ran out. A Nazi bullet killed her. She was dead at eighteen, a beautiful flower cut down by the cruel hand of our enemy.

But life had to go on. My father, who had been appointed a platoon leader, was busy performing his duties. He, too, was grieving, but he tried his best to get on with his life and duties. When we visited my mother, he would hold Sheindale in his arms, and talk to her softly. He tried his best to fill in for my mother who was unable to do anything in those first terrible days after Dina's death. I, too, found out that the daily routine eased some of my pain and I did what I could to go on with my life.

Time is a great healer. Little by little, my mother emerged from her mourning. She spent a lot of time with Sheindale and tried to help the others who needed her. It seemed as though she tried to find a new meaning in her life. She talked often with Yonah, trying to help him to overcome his pain at the loss of Dina, his love.

As the winter progressed, news from the front was getting better and better. The Russian Army was coming closer to our part of the Ukraine. We were told that by spring we would be liberated.

Spring came. For two weeks we heard the artillery shots getting closer and closer. After a long series of battles, in which some units of our brigade took part, the Russian soldiers came. At last the war was over for us. The Germans were defeated, and we were liberated.

I will never forget the look on Sheindale's face when a Russian soldier gave her a spoonful of sugar to spread on her bread. This was the first time since we were taken from our home that she tasted sugar. She most certainly enjoyed it.

As long as the fighting went on, we could not leave our partisan brigade. But now we had a future, a chance to live as free human beings despite the fact that we could not yet go back to our home. This was to come later, in the summer, when all of the Ukraine was liberated.

12

The Rescue Of A Jewish Child

In early spring of 1944, the war was over for us, but the fighting was still going on all over Europe. In fact the rest of the world was still hard at war until May 8, 1945.

After our liberation, most of the men in the partisan brigade were drafted into the Russian Army. Some went to the front while others were engaged in local mop-up jobs, mostly going after collaborators and bringing them to justice. My father and I were told that we were no longer needed for military service and that we were free to return home. Uncle Moshe continued to serve as a soldier in the local Red Army unit.

Our whole family and some of the members of our group, among them my Uncle Moshe, our friends Leibl and Yosl, were able to obtain passes on the train going to our shtetl, Malinsk. Before leaving the family camp, my mother asked to be taken to the place in the forest where my sister Dina was buried. There she said a last goodbye to her beloved daughter, not knowing if we would ever be able to return for her body.

Our life as partisans in the forest was finally over. We picked up our bundles and set out for home. After an absence of more than two and a half years, we were back in Malinsk.

But was this still our home? Our farm was now occupied by Russian soldiers and declared off limits to civilians. We were instructed to find a place to live in the shtetl proper. This proved to be impossible. Ukrainians now occupied all the houses.

We were the only Jewish family that survived and returned to the shtetl. All around us we saw that the homes of our dead friends were now occupied by strangers. And we saw the looks of hatred on the faces of the new occupants of those homes.

Memories of our own beloved murdered family members and our friends were so overpowering that the pain was unbearable. It became very clear to us that Malinsk was no longer our home. We had to go elsewhere, to a place where other Jewish survivors lived. Once again, we picked up our bundles, boarded the train and went to Rovno.

Rovno was a city in ruins. Most of the buildings were destroyed by the battles that had raged in the area. With some luck, we were able to locate a vacant house that sustained only minimal damage from a mortar shell, and we settled in it. All the glass panes in the windows were broken, but this did not really matter to us because it was getting warmer each day. The house had a kitchen with a wood burning stove and two small rooms.

For us, it was a luxury to live in a house, sleep on a bed, cook in a kitchen, have a well in the backyard from which we could draw fresh clean water. By bartering some of the goods that my parents managed to retrieve from their hiding places in Malinsk, we were able to acquire some basic furniture and kitchen utensils.

We were settling into a seemingly normal way of life. My mother began talking about my going back to school, about Sheindale starting first grade in September. Her grief over the death of my older sister was constantly there, but the needs of her living children, as well as the needs of other survivors, took precedence and helped to ease some of her pain. Within a very short time, the word was out that in Rovno, on Kamini Street lived a Jewish family; a father, a mother, and two children. It was such a rarity for a family unit to have survived that it was almost a miracle. Many of the Jewish survivors who arrived in Rovno came to our house. Somehow, my mother managed to cook enough soup to feed all of our visitors. Somehow, a clean shirt was given to a man without a shirt, a pair of shoes found for a young woman.

Most of the people who came to our house were the only surviving members of their own families, having lost parents, sisters, brothers, wives, husbands, and children. They came and seemed to take comfort from their contact with a Jewish family, consisting of parents and children, just like their own families used to be. It was as though this contact gave them the strength to continue living.

Each survivor had a miraculous story of survival to tell – stories of close brushes with death and survival due to luck at a crucial moment, which determined one's fate. Each survivor lived through a unique experience different from the experiences of all the others. Each had a personal perspective on what went on in the particular part of the forest where he hid. The stories told were as diverse as the survivors who told them.

People would come, stay with us a day, or two, or more, before continuing on their way. Before leaving, they would write their names in a notebook, which my mother kept. This was done to inform others of their survival, and serve as a contact point for any relatives of theirs who might have survived the war, and who might come to our house.

Life in Rovno after the war was not easy. There was very little food in the city and everything was rationed. Laborers received special food rations. My father found a job as a dispatcher in the train yard. I was enrolled to start high school in September.

Meanwhile, I had more important things to do. Father's job allowed me free access to train passes. As there was practically no food to be obtained in the city, I used to hop on a train going to some small rural village down the line where I traded with the farmers, bartering tobacco, which I bought in Rovno with my father's ration card, for food. In this way, I was able to obtain food for my family and for the many people who ate at our table. If we wanted to survive, this was the only way of obtaining food.

Trading was a dangerous thing to do for two reasons. First, being a Jewish boy among Ukrainian farmers was not safe. To safeguard against this deeply ingrained hatred, I assumed once more the role of a Ukrainian boy, but this time I presented myself as a city boy, who needed to take care of his mother and sister. The second reason was that it was against Russian law to buy food illegally from the farmers. The authorities denounced this activity. It was seen as engaging in black-market activity, a crime punishable by a long term in prison.

I felt that there was no choice. I had to come home with food for my family, and trading was the only way to do it.

I was not the only one trading for food, either. I was trading on a small scale, but others did it on a larger scale, as a business. They were really in trouble if caught by the police.

I had a few close calls with the Russian police, but I managed to get away. My father realized the danger I faced and tried to dissuade me from continuing this dangerous occupation, but I kept doing it, because we needed the food, and because it was exciting. After my experience as a fighting partisan, it wasn't easy for me to get used to a normal, quiet life – the life of a typical schoolboy.

Little did I know that very soon, our quiet life would again change.

One day a young woman came to our house. She asked to speak to my father. We invited her to wait until he returned from work. My mother conversed with her, while serving her tea and tried to find out something about her and her reason for wanting to talk to my father. The woman said that her name was Leah, and that she was from Klevan, a small shtetl in the vicinity of Rovno, but she persisted in not giving mother any other information about herself. She would talk about her problem only with my father. This was quite unusual. Most of the survivors who showed up at our doorstep were very eager to talk, to tell what happened to them. They especially liked to talk with my mother, who was a sympathetic listener. It was as though they derived some comfort in telling about their own survival, or talking about their beloved family members who perished.

Some time later, Sheindale, who was playing in the backyard, walked into the kitchen. When Leah saw her, she started sobbing and tears ran down her cheeks. She kept murmuring "My daughter, my daughter." My mother tried to comfort her and Sheindale came over and stood next to her saying, "Don't cry. Please don't cry." Eventually Leah stopped crying, but did not speak. At the end of the workday, father came home and after we ate dinner, Leah finally told us her story and the problem she faced. We sat very quietly and listened to her without interrupting.

"I grew up and lived all my life in a shtetl that had a small number of Jewish inhabitants. I did not look Jewish, being fair, blue eyed and blond. I spoke Ukrainian and Russian very well, without any accent and could easily pass as a gentile.

In 1940, I married my beloved husband Chaim. Despite the war and the Russian occupation, we were very happy. Our happiness was made complete when our baby daughter Chayale, who resembled me, was born. By the time the Nazis occupied our shtetl, she was almost a year old. The Nazis took my husband to a work camp, and I never saw him again. I learned about his death only after liberation.

We, the women and children of the shtetl, were moved to an enclosed area of the shtetl. It was not a real ghetto and most of the time we could come and go freely, but we knew that we were not free. Food was very scarce and I had a feeling that the situation would get worse. I knew that my baby would not survive in the ghetto. I realized that I must save my daughter and try to save myself. All the time I had hoped that my husband would be able to escape from the camp and come back to us, but this never happened.

I decided to pass myself off as a Ukrainian and find a safe place for my baby and myself. But as time went by and I could not find safety for both of us, I decided that I had no other choice but to find shelter for my baby in some gentile home and leave her there for the duration of the war.

Once she was safe, I could find a safe place for myself. Parting from my beloved baby was a very hard decision for me to make, but I had no choice. Even so, I had very little time to accomplish my plan.

I took my baby to a nearby village, Bronniki, where a Ukrainian family, the Polanows, lived. They used to come to my father's store, sell their produce and buy dry goods from him. I knew that they were friendly people, who seemed to like Jews so I decided to leave my baby with them. Before leaving the ghetto, I wrote a note in Ukrainian saying, "Good people, save this baby, treat her as your own, and may God bless you."

I attached this note and my wedding ring to the baby's blanket and walked to the village where they lived. In the evening when it turned dark, I put my sleeping baby on their doorstep, and hid a little distance away. From a distance, I stood guard over my sleeping baby until dawn when she woke up and started crying. The farmer opened the door, saw the bundle on the doorstep, picked my baby up, and took her inside. I stayed hidden, trying to ascertain what would happen, to make sure that my baby was safe. In the late afternoon, the farmer and his wife, carrying my baby, walked out of the house, and went toward another house, a short distance away. They stayed in that house for a while, and then walked back to their home, without my baby.

I could not stay in my hiding place any longer. When there was no one around, I left and walked back to my shtetl without my child, crying bitterly all the way. It's the cruelest thing in the world for a mother to have to give away her child.

After two days, I walked back to Bronniki, where I had left my baby. I had to find out where she was and what happened to her. In the village, I asked for the schoolteacher's house and went there. In any Ukrainian village, there were a few people who knew everything about its inhabitants. The priest, the policeman, and the schoolteacher were among them. I realized that contacting the schoolteacher was the safest way for me to find out what I needed to know. I met the teacher and told him a fictional story about myself, about needing a place to stay, and to find work. Then I asked him some questions about the Polanows, after giving him a reasonable pretext for my curiosity. The teacher believed my story and asked, "Which of the Polanows are you asking about, Is it Pawel, or his sister-in-law, Sonia, the wife of Anton?" Something made me say that I needed to hear about Anton Polanow because my husband knew him.

"It is a very sad story," the teacher said, "Anton was taken by the retreating Russian soldiers, and poor Sonia, his wife, was left all alone. She is a good Christian woman, neat and hard-working, but very lonely, having no children."

He stopped talking, then continued, "Just the other day, I heard that a relative of hers from Rovno entrusted her with the care of her baby because there is no food in the city. Now Sonia will not feel so alone. This little baby will give her comfort until God brings back her husband and gives her a baby of her own."

He kept on talking, telling me that there was no work to be found in this village, but in the outlying farms, a strong and hard-working woman might find work and a place to stay. I listened to his good advice, but most of all, I felt secure because my plan worked and my baby was safe and in good hands. I thanked him for his help and left.

Now the way was open for me to find a safe haven for myself. I managed to pass myself off successfully as a Christian. Eventually I found shelter as a farm worker on an outlying farm. I stayed on the farm until the Germans were defeated.

All this time, I kept myself informed about Sonia Polanow and my baby. I used to go on Sunday to the church in the village for Sunday services. I would see my little girl, sitting next to Sonia during prayers. How I longed to hug and kiss her, but I knew that this was impossible.

After liberation, I walked to Bronniki and went to Sonia Polanow's house. I thanked Sonia from the bottom of my heart for saving my baby, who by now was four years old. I told her the truth about leaving my baby on the doorsteps of her relatives, the Polanows. "I am the mother of this little girl. Now that the danger is over, I want to take her back," I said. I offered to pay her for taking care of my baby all these years. When Sonia heard the real story of how this little baby came to her, she became very agitated. She accused me of being a liar, wanting to take away her own child from her. She would not listen to reason. She chased me out of her house, not allowing me to see or talk to my little girl. I left, but decided to come the next day to take my Chayale. I needed to get my daughter back.

When I came the following day, there was no one in Sonia's house. It was locked and looked deserted. I left the house and came back the next day and the day after that, but Sonia and my child had disappeared. I made some discreet inquiries, paid for some information, and found out eventually that Sonia took my child to a small convent, some distance away, and left her there.

Maybe I was to blame for what happened. Now, I realize that I was too hasty, and did not take into account that Sonia had grown to love my daughter. But the driving reason for what I did was the fact that she is my daughter. I love her and want her back. She is my flesh and blood. She is all that is left to me in this world.

I went to the convent and asked for a meeting with the Mother Superior. I told her my story. She acknowledged that the child, Maria Polanow, was indeed in the convent, but she was a Christian child who had the baptismal papers to prove that this was the truth. According to the Mother Superior, the little girl was left in the convent while her mother went to Russia to look for her missing husband. The Mother Superior forbade me to come again to the convent.

During the time that I argued with her, I had the feeling that she knew that I was telling the truth, but chose to ignore it and to help Sonia Polanow.

"It is well known that many times the churches issued fake baptismal certificates in order to prove that the person was a Christian to help save them from the Nazis. But in this case, she was helping to keep my daughter from me."

Now, my Chayale is still in the convent, in Cameljana, but I do not know how long she will stay there. They might move her to another convent, and I will lose track of her. I need to act as quickly as possible to get my daughter back before it is too late. This is why I come to you, begging for your help, Hershl Fein. I heard that you are a brave man, a partisan, and that you are willing to help Jews who are in need of help. I need your help. I must get my child back. She is all that I have left in this world. So, please, help me."

This was not the first time we heard that parents, trying to save their children, left them on the doorsteps of Ukrainian farmers. They hoped that mercy for these small unfortunate children would persuade the farmers to give them a safe home. In some cases, surviving parents have been able to get their children back easily. In other instances, they have had to resort to violence to get them back. We have heard that there are still many Jewish children who haven't been claimed, probably because their parents did not survive. These children will never learn their true identity.

Upon hearing Leah's story, my father did not answer right away. He sat, deep in thought, as we watched him in silence. Finally, he looked at Sheindale, who sat next to him, then he looked at my mother, then at Leah, and said, "Every Jewish mother deserves to have her child with her. As long as they both are alive, they must be reunited. Leah, I promise you that I will do my best to help you. You are right, a Jewish partisan does not only fight the Nazis, but he also helps his own people."

Turning to me he said, "Benny, we must move fast. We need four or five good men for this mission. Uncle Moshe, Leibl Schneider, Yosl Kaplan, and the two of us can do the job. We also need guns for a show of strength. Moshe will be here soon and I will fill him in about this operation. Go find the others. At this time of the day, they are all back from work. Tell them to come here immediately."

I did not need any additional prodding. I ran from our house to the apartment where Yosl and Leibl lived. I found them at home and asked them to come to our house to talk with father.

When we were all assembled, father introduced Leah to them, and in a few short words outlined her request. Without hesitating, they all agreed to help her.

A plan was formulated. Leibl and Uncle Moshe would supply the needed guns. Father would arrange train passes for us. We would take the train to the village closest to the convent, wait until dusk, go in and rescue the child. Once we had the little girl, we would split into two groups. The first, including my father, Leah, Chayale and I, would go cross-country to a train station farther up the track, where only freight trains stop during the night. This station was some distance from the convent. We would try to catch the midnight freight train back to Rovno. We must look like a regular family trying to get to the big city, for a day, to do some marketing. The other men would walk in the opposite direction, down the track, and return by passenger train to Rovno.

"Wait, wait," my mother said. "Chayale has never seen any of you. She will be frightened. She will cry. This will put you all in danger." She was right, as usual.

Then my mother had an idea. "I will go over to visit my friend, a pharmacist. I will tell her that Sheindale has a toothache and ask her for a sleeping powder to help her fall asleep. I'll say that she has a very badly infected tooth, but the dentist will only be able to see her the next day."

My mother left to get the sleeping powder and we kept discussing our plans for the next day.

We decided that once inside the convent, we would keep our faces covered at all times, to protect our identities. We also decided that Leah would not come into the convent because she might be recognized. Under no circumstances were the guns to be used. We would have them just to frighten the nuns and help us to get Chayale out of there. We knew that this was a dangerous undertaking, and if caught, we might pay dearly.

By the time my mother got back, holding small white paper envelopes in her hand, our plans were finalized. We were to meet at the train station, get our passes from father, and keep away from each other until we reached our destination. "At all costs, we are to stay separate until the last moment, because a group of five men traveling together will draw suspicion," my father said.

I was very exited about the whole plan. I was very proud of my father, uncle, and friends. Above all, it was good to be counted as a man who was expected to take full part in this action.

The next day, at noon, we met, and proceeded to carry out our plan. It all worked fine, with one exception. At the last moment, we decided that Leah would go to the convent. We realized that we needed her to gain entry, since the nuns would not allow strange men inside. We also needed her to identify Chayale for us.

Since Leah would be the number one suspect in the abduction, she had to do her part and then go into hiding for a while. According to the new plan, once we had Chayale, Leah would go back to Rovno with the other men, while father and I would take the little girl with us, after giving her some of the medicated milk to drink. We would pretend that she was sick, and that we were taking her to the hospital in Rovno. Once there, we would bring her to our house, and mother would take care of her for a while.

Our plan worked without a hitch. We arrived at the convent after dusk, as planned. Leah knocked on the heavy wooden door, and once it was opened, we barged in, waving our guns, faces covered, just like real bandits, who at that time still roamed the country, seeking to make an easy living by robbing other peoples' treasures. The only treasure we wanted was one little Jewish girl.

The nuns cowered fearfully at our display of power. Leah told one of them to show her where Maria Polanow slept. She told the nun to wake the girl gently so as not to alarm her, to dress her, and tell her that she was being taken to meet her mother. She was also to have the little girl drink milk from the bottle Leah gave her. The nun complied without saying much, but her eyes spoke volumes. I was sure that if she had a gun in her hand, she would have shot us without hesitation.

Chayale, who was half asleep anyway, did not give us any trouble. She drank the milk, and dozed off. Leah wrapped her daughter in a warm blanket, took her in her arms and walked out of the convent. We kept our guns trained on the nuns until she was out the door and some distance from the convent. Leibl told the nuns to close the door and stay put. "I will stay outside, and keep watch. If one of you tries to leave the convent, I'll shoot."

As planned, we split into two parties, an elated Leah and three men going one way, and father and I, carrying the little girl, going in the opposite direction. We were happy that our plan had worked thus far. One more dangerous part still awaited us, but we hoped that at midnight nobody would pay any attention to us.

Chayale slept, snoring lightly. Our cover story was good, and if no alarm was given, we could complete the journey without trouble.

After a very long walk, we reached the train station a short time before the train was due. To our surprise, there were a number of Russian policemen at the station. They went from one group of passengers to another, asking them to open their bundles for inspection. For a few anxious moments, we were very nervous. Could the alarm about the abduction of the little girl already have been given? Were they looking for us? Those were questions that ran through my mind. "Act naturally and don't show any panic," my father whispered, walking directly toward a policeman. "Comrade policeman, can you tell us if the train will be on time tonight? My little girl is sick. I am taking her to the hospital," he said in Ukrainian. The policeman looked at us, lifted the blanket gently from Chayale's sleeping face and said, "It is all right. Don't worry, the train will be on time."

We were very relieved. They were not looking for us. They were intent on catching farmers who brought their produce to sell in the black-market and were guilty of breaking the law. The police caught a few farmers who had a large quantity of food and took them aside for further questioning.

When the train arrived, we boarded and found a place to sit on the dirty floor – and thanked God for our good luck.

Chayale slept throughout the journey and kept on sleeping for a few more hours at our house. I walked over to Leibl's apartment to let him know that we made it home safely. Leah was staying with some other friends, and word was sent to her that all was well.

When Chayale woke up, she was very scared and kept crying and asking for her mother, of course meaning Sonia, who was the only mother she had ever known. It took a lot of patience and love to calm her down. For some reason, she took to me right away, and kept asking me to pick her up, and tell her a story. I think this helped her feel more secure with us. It was lucky that I had some experience as an older brother and knew how to entertain her. Sheindale was also a great help. She played with Chayale, who still insisted that her name was Maria.

After about a week, Leah finally came to see her daughter, bringing her chocolates and a new doll. My mother told her to be very patient with Chayale, to go slowly, and gain her affection and trust, step by step because one problem still remained and had to be resolved. Chayale was very frightened of going near the bath tub. Chayale told my mother that her mother, Sonia, warned her that the Jewish people would try to hurt her, maybe even try to drown her. So with a tremendous amount of love from my mother and Leah, Chayale began to forget Sonia's warning and finally allowed Leah to give her a bath. Time proved to be the best healer.

The day came when Leah asked Chayale to call her mama, and Chayale did so. Now we knew they were ready to be together.

Our last mission as Jewish partisans was a success. We left no traces behind us. We heard of no official complaint to the authorities about the abduction of a little girl from the convent. If Sonia did search for her missing ward, we never heard about it.

Epilogue

We were having dinner one evening when suddenly, gunfire erupted all around us. We were startled! What happened? Who was shooting? Had the Germans attacked us, or were we being attacked by Ukrainian Nationalists who were opposed to the Russian regimen? Sheindale started crying. Mother's face turned pale from shock. We did not know whether to take shelter or get our guns?

We ran to the windows to see what was going on. Looking at the brilliant sky, we saw the most beautiful display of fireworks imaginable. We heard people cheering, "Hurrah! Hurrah! The war is over. Germany surrendered!"

We walked out of the house, toward the main street. Everyone was in the street. The explosions went on and on, but we knew that it was not gunfire, but fireworks. People were hugging and kissing. Some had bottles of vodka in their hands, which they shared willingly with passersby. Others were singing Russian songs.

"Germany surrendered! Hitler is dead! We won! We won!" they kept repeating to each other as though unable to believe their own ears.

Somehow a group of us, Jewish partisans who fought the Nazis, drifted together. With tears in our eyes, we marveled at this wonderful scene – peace – for which we prayed for, for so long. Someone started singing softly in Yiddish the famous partisan song, *"Zog nit keyn mol az du geyst dem letstn veg* – Do not ever say that you are going on the last journey." We all joined in. This was a song of defiance, hope and victory, and it ended with the words *"Mir zaynen du*! – We are here!"

This was the best moment of my whole life. If only Dina, Shlomo, and the others could have been here with us to celebrate.

After celebrating the end of the war, a window of opportunity to leave the Ukraine opened up for us. All Polish citizens were allowed to leave. The members of our family were officially registered as Polish citizens, so we requested permission to go to Poland. After some time and paying some hefty bribes to Russian officials, permission was granted.

We made our way to Lodz and then to a Displaced Persons camp in Germany. My parents knew that Europe could never be our home. It was soaked with so much Jewish blood.

For a long time, they discussed their dream of going to live in Palestine. They wanted to go to the ancient Jewish homeland, to begin a new life in the Land of Israel. "Only there will we truly be at home and live among other Jews, far from bitter memories and hate," my mother said. We agreed with her.

Once more, we packed our meager possessions and set out on the long, long journey to our only real home – the Land of Israel.